RUSSIA IN TRANSITION, 1905–1914

RUSSIA IN TRANSITION 1905–1914

Evolution or Revolution?

Edited by ROBERT H. McNEAL
University of Massachusetts

HOLT, RINEHART AND WINSTON
New York · Chicago · San Francisco · Atlanta
Dallas · Montreal · Toronto · London · Sydney

Cover illustration: Veterans of the Revolution of 1905 on parade in Red Square, Moscow, November 1939. (*Sovfoto*)

CONTENTS

INTRODUCTION

The twentieth century has been an age of severe stress for most societies and governments. Relatively few countries have not changed their form of government at least once during the century, and all have gone through periods of extreme social and economic difficulty. For the student of history, one of the most important problems for analysis is determining the difference between an impending revolutionary crack-up, which cannot really be a chronic situation in any country, and a condition of serious difficulty, which is common and often sustained. Although the study of some decade in the twentieth-century history of almost any country would reveal numerous diseases of the body politic, these would not necessarily lead to revolution. The historian (and observer of his own day) must seek to distinguish between incipient revolution and evolution through travail. Otherwise he will run the risk of detecting doom with absurd regularity or of failing to understand the sources of the great outbursts that do occur.

The Russian empire between the Revolution of 1905 and the outbreak of World War I in 1914 presents an unusually interesting problem in this regard. During that vital period in the development of a superpower, a tense confrontation occurred between Europe's most hated conservative government and the most militant radical movement in Europe. We know now that a faction of the radical movement emerged victorious in 1917, and this no doubt heightens our interest in the situation between 1904 and 1914. The double revolution in Russia in 1917 does not, however, establish that the Russian empire was on the verge of internal collapse and turmoil before it entered its final ordeal by combat. World War I did happen, and there is general agreement that by 1916, if not earlier, it had a deleterious effect on the stability of the old order. The question is, did it ruin a potentiality for nonrevolutionary modernization, or did the war merely bring an inexorable ailment to its crisis?

Historians are sharply divided on this matter. To some extent the debate is between Soviet Communist historians and non-Communists. Soviet historians are all committed to the conclusion that the Revolution of 1917 was a demonstration of the general laws of history which Marx ascertained and Lenin elaborated concerning the imperialist stage of capitalism in the twentieth century. The Soviet historians are obliged to find the last years of the Russian empire a time of repeated revolutionary crises, the first, in 1905 to 1907, followed by an interlude of enforced pacification, then by a new upsurge, in 1912 to 1914, interrupted by World War I, and finally by the decisive uprising in 1917. If this framework were the only mandatory premise for Soviet historians, it would still leave considerable room for individual variation, but there are further constraints. Lenin, the founder of the Soviet Communist party, was both a participant in and a prolific commentator on Russian politics from 1905 to 1914, and the party still obliges Soviet historians to accept many specific opinions that he expressed in those years. They must perpetuate all of Lenin's obsessively partisan appraisals of his rivals among the opponents of the imperial regime—liberals, Menshevik socialists (Marxists), and Socialist Revolutionaries (agrarian socialists). After the passage of sixty years, one might expect that Soviet writers could at least do justice to Trotsky's dramatic leadership of the Petrograd Soviet, a concession that would not detract at all from the general Marxist thesis about the disintegration of the old order. But no, Lenin's rival in 1905 must be punished to the *n*th generation.

No non-Communist historian accepts all the details of Soviet works on the last years of the empire, with their sectarian bias. But several distinguished non-Communist students of the period accept the general view that by 1914 the Russian Empire was sliding toward disaster. Leopold Haimson, an authority on the Mensheviks, concludes that there is much to be said for the Bolshevik thesis on impending revolt. Theodore H. Von Laue reached a similar conclusion on the basis of careful study of imperial government policy, especially in the field of industrialization.

The choice, then, between a pessimistic and an optimistic appraisal of the situation in Russia in 1905 to 1914 need *not* be a response to the official Marxist-Leninist interpretation. There is certainly more than one alternative to the general thesis that the empire was on the path to disintegration in 1914. The more optimistic historians may variously emphasize the development of representative institutions, the strength of the government's civil and military forces, the progress of agriculture and industry, the rapid advance of mass education, or the democratization of society. Alternatively, the reader of the diverse arguments may be impressed with the serious liabilities of the imperial order, but may feel that the case for incipient revolution deserves a verdict sometimes rendered by Scottish courts: not proved.

Varied as these opinions may be, there is substantial agreement that the following developments are relevant and deserve analysis: the Revolution of 1905, the new legislative and executive institutions that followed from it, the agrarian reform associated with the name of Premier Stolypin, the growth of industry, and the situation that had emerged by the eve of World War I. The readings in this book illustrate the major arguments that have been put forward concerning each of these aspects of the general problem.

Both Soviet and Western historians observed the fiftieth anniversary of the Revolution of 1905 with essays appraising its place in Russian history. This subject is considered in the first two selections in this study, which were written in 1955 and have some important features in common. Both Oskar Anweiler, a West German professor, and the anonymous author of the selection from the Soviet publication *Historical Transactions* attach great importance to this revolution. Not all historians do so. Sergei Pushkarev, for example, takes a fairly optimistic view of the Russian empire from 1905 to 1914, and minimizes the severity and impact of the first Russian revolution. One major proponent of the pessimistic interpretation of the period, Von Laue, treats it as a passing squall.

Anweiler and Soviet scholars, however, speak of the revolution of 1905–1907, calling attention to the considerable duration of the upheaval. In their opinion, it was finally quelled only when Premier Stolypin dissolved the Second Duma and revised the electoral laws in June 1907. They perceive this protracted struggle as a major turning point in Russian history, almost on a par with 1917. There is also agreement between Anweiler and the Soviet interpretation in identifying the main sources of revolutionary power: industrial strikes, the formation of soviets, peasant uprisings, mutiny in the armed forces, and rebellious national minorities.

Despite this common ground, the two interpretations reach completely different conclusions about the meaning of the revolution of 1905–1907. Anweiler regards it as the end of an era of political and social obsolescence and rigidity, and the beginning of a period of "open possibilities." Rejecting any assumptions about the inevitability of proletarian revolution, he holds that the first Russian revolution should be studied as a turning point in its own right, not as a preparation for 1917.

The Leninist version of Marxism, represented by the essay from *Historical Transactions,* is based on a general conception of history: the decay of capitalism in its final, fatal stage of imperialism, which precedes the socialist revolution and final solution to man's problems. If this Leninist thesis is accepted as the pattern of modern history, how do the main events of Russian history in the twentieth century fit into it? Russia in 1905, with its relatively underdeveloped economy and its autocratic government, is considered to be on the verge of the bourgeois-democratic revolution, *not* the proletarian revolution. But Lenin was never content to see the despised liberals lead a united front of the opponents of the old order. He maintained that the proletariat, however small in numbers, had to lead the first revolution because the Russian bourgeois liberals were unwilling to consummate it. In doing so the proletariat was preparing the country and itself for the final, socialist revolution. On this basis Soviet historians have often called the revolution of 1905–1907 a dress rehearsal for 1917.

The first two readings in the second group of selections are devoted mainly to the new representative institution of Russia, the duma. Note that Paul Miliukov, a leading Russian liberal, and Sir Bernard Pares, a liberal English historian of Russia, deal with the First and Second Dumas, in 1906–1907, mainly as constitutional history, not as part of a revolution. Like certain other writers in the liberal tradition, they tend to bring down the curtain on the Revolution of 1905 with the suppression of the Moscow uprising in December of that year. Thenceforth their interest is mainly in the parliamentary politics that were made possible by the autocracy's concessions. Miliukov's principal concern is the First Duma, even though it lasted only about two months (May-July 1907). This emphasis is partly explained by the fact that Miliukov's own party, the Constitutional Democrats (Kadets), had the largest representation and played the leading role in this duma (though Miliukov himself was disqualified from standing for election because he did not fulfill a residence requirement at the time). His approach is not simply an expression of party prejudice. For many Russian liberals, the great opportunity of 1906 was the possibility of establishing responsible government, of subordinating the executive (the ministers) to the people's representatives. Not without reason, they deemed this to be a necessary foundation for successful constitutional monarchy. For Miliukov, the great disaster of 1906–1907 was not the decline of violent revolution but the government's rejection of the prospect of a parliamentary, constitutional monarchy. But Sir Bernard Pares, steeped in the British idea of political compromise and gradualism, is quite willing to see the Third Duma as a redemption of liberalism, despite its undemocratic election. His message might be paraphrased, the Third Duma *worked*—and is it not sensible to teach elected representatives and the ministers to cooperate first and worry about parliamentary supremacy and democratic elections later?

Both of these variants on the liberal interpretation of the postrevolutionary political scene encounter challenges from the Left and the Right. The Soviet historian Aron Iakovlevich Avrekh, following a major tradition of Marxism, finds it instructive that the liberals are inclined to de-emphasize the revolutionary content of the period, while speaking much of the duma. Most historians probably agree that Marxism has a point in asserting that liberals do not make the most thoroughgoing revolutionaries. Non-Marxists may argue that this is so because liberals seek the peaceful, parliamentary solution of public issues, when at all possible. Avrekh, in the Marxist tradition, has another answer: liberals are bourgeois and fear revolution because of the economic interest of their class, even though they may occasionally timidly exploit revolutionary postures to frighten the old regime. On this basis Avrekh builds his picture of the Third Duma as a cabal between the bourgeoisie and Premier Stolypin. If the liberals tend to minimize evidence of popular revolutionary feeling, Soviet historians, including Avrekh, have remarkably little to say about the intransigence of Russian liberals toward the government, including Stolypin. It is not easy to square the theory of a bourgeois deal with the autocracy and the firm evidence that both the Kadets (represented by Miliukov) and the Octobrists (favored by Pares) rejected invitations to join the council of ministers (that is, the cabinet).

Yet this is what happened, and Leonid I. Strakhovsky, who stands opposite Avrekh in the political spectrum, finds this deliberate denial of liberal cooperation a most serious blow to the political renewal envisaged by Stolypin. The Marxist charge of a liberal sellout to tsarism is balanced by a conservative charge of sabotage by the liberals. Strakhovsky's essay may be read as an exceptionally undiluted version of the interpretation that sees in Premier Stolypin the most promising combination of strength and reform. Even if one does not wish to go as far as Strakhovsky, it is clear that Stolypin was the central figure within the government in this period. Not even most admirers of Nicholas II are inclined to suggest that the tsar was capable personally of being a strong chief executive—a function he had in some measure delegated to his premier in 1905. Stolypin was the only man in this post who perhaps came close to realizing its potentialities.

His name is associated particularly with the most ambitious government undertaking of these years: the agrarian reform. In a country that was still predominantly agricultural, this reform could be the crucial factor, and any analyst of the state of the empire must take into account its success or failure. The third group of selections, which centers on problems of the economy, opens with a discussion of the agrarian reform.

While Strakhovsky finds the goals of the reform valid and progress toward them impressive, the Soviet historian S. M. Dubrovsky disagrees on both counts. Following Lenin, he sees the policy of Stolypin as an attempt to transform Russian agriculture on the "Prussian" model. Lenin maintained that there were two main forms of capitalist agriculture, the Prussian type, in which the former feudal landlords operate large, modern farms, and the American type, characterized by relatively small private farms. In view of Stolypin's expressed aim of assisting the "strong" peasants (sometimes interpreted as meaning a minority of kulaks, but actually meaning the majority of the peasant class), one might suppose that he tended more toward the American pattern.

But Dubrovsky insists that this was not so, that government policy was fundamentally controlled by feudal landlords *(krepostniki-pomeshchiki)*, whose interest in assisting some kulaks (literally "fists," a colloquial term for well-to-do peasants) was secondary to their interest in expanding capitalist-landlord agriculture. In other words, the government tried to forestall democratic revolution in the countryside by gaining the loyalty of a minority of well-to-do peasants; and Stolypin tried at the same time to serve the interests of the rich landlords. Such an antidemocratic policy could be pursued only by coercion. Dubrovsky concludes that despite its ruthlessness the government did not succeed in establishing any significant body of peasant support. Like the Bonapartist policy of Stolypin in politics, the Prussian policy in agriculture faced the specter of revolution.

Dubrovsky's premises are not shared by George L. Yaney, who specializes in the study of Russian imperial policy making and administration. Yaney argues that the concept of the Stolypin reform was not a simple one of assisting kulaks or landlords. Accepting the good faith of the leading bureaucrats concerning peasant welfare, Yaney thinks that these officials worked pragmatically to find ways and means of modernizing the countryside which were acceptable to the peasants. In the selection reprinted here he does not attempt to analyze economically the results of the reform, but the impression is that one should not discount the competence and reasonableness of the administrators in dealing with peasant problems, or the willingness of the peasants to cooperate with these efforts.

Concentrating on the agrarian economics of the reform, W. E. Mosse reaches less favorable conclusions. His analysis of the impact of the Stolypin legislation attempts to take into account the social and regional diversity of Russian agrarian conditions, and he acknowledges that it enjoyed success in some areas among some elements of the peasantry, but his evaluation of the net result is negative. Most particularly, Mosse believes that time was not on the side of the reform, that the pace of the transformation of the Russian rural scene from traditional communalism to presumably more modern individualism was far too slow to be a basis for optimism concerning the fate of the Russian empire.

While Mosse's assumption seems to be that the peasant question can best be treated as an autonomous feature of Russian life, the economic historian Alexander Gerschenkron treats the Stolypin reform in the context of the general problem of economic development, placing particular emphasis on the relation of the peasant to industrialization. In his view the freeing of peasants from their traditional communal ties was one of the major prerequisites for the rapid industrial advance that Russia experienced in the years following the Revolution of 1905. Nobody contests that there was such an advance, or a revival of the industrial growth that had marked the 1890s and had entered a slump at the beginning of the twentieth century, but there is considerable argument concerning its political and social significance. Gerschenkron maintains that it was a relatively mature and stable development which reflected the increased availability of domestic capital and managerial talent, along with some diffusion of prosperity. In his interpretation the reviving strike movement in 1912–1914 signifies a trade-unionist tendency to improve the workers' standard of living rather than incipient revolution.

The final group of selections presents alternative views of the condition of the Russian empire in 1914: was it on the verge of disintegration, or was it coping with the problems of modernization? In this section we encounter two attempts to convince the reader that one verdict or the other has been proved. The writers of two other essays are not convinced that a simple decision is now possible for the judicious historian.

The authors of the official Communist textbook on party history, edited by party Secretary Boris N. Ponomarev, sum up the case for the prosecution: the empire had not fundamentally strengthened its position since 1905 and was on the verge of revolution before the war broke out. While recognizing, with Gerschenkron and others, that Russian industry was growing rapidly just before the war, the Communist historians regard this as a source of additional stress. The larger the industrial proletariat, the stronger the army of revolution.

This argument assumes that the urban workers became increasingly militant and well organized. Naturally enough, the official historians of the Communist party, the heirs of Lenin, believe that the desired state of revolutionary preparedness could only be achieved under Bolshevik leadership. Other self-styled opponents of the regime, such as the Mensheviks, can only be considered fakes who betrayed the proletariat and wished to liquidate the Russian Social Democratic

Party. The reader who was not raised on such a diet may well be inclined to dismiss Ponomarev's case as propaganda. But it is generally accepted that there was a growing wave of strikes, and there is no doubt at all that the violent strike of July 1914 in Petersburg had to be suppressed by the army. As previously mentioned, a number of non-Soviet historians have concluded that the Soviet case, minus its sectarian rhetoric, has much substance. (In reaching this conclusion the non-Soviet historians also discount at least one broad generalization that appears in the selection from the Communist textbook: that Russian industry was lagging further and further behind that of the advanced countries. This assertion cannot be substantiated by production statistics for the major industries, and most Soviet historians do not subscribe to it.)

Knowing that Lenin and the Bolsheviks eventually did come to power in Russia, it might at first glance seem natural and not very controversial to identify them with the cause of revolution in the pre-World War I era, as does the Soviet historian Ponomarev. But this appraisal of the prehistory of the Communist party of the Soviet Union does not by any means go unchallenged. Harold Shukman sums up an alternative interpretation that is widely held by historians in the West. While paying tribute to Lenin's unremittingly aggressive militancy, Shukman also calls attention to the weaknesses of the Bolsheviks as a would-be vanguard of proletarian revolution. He finds that Lenin's ideological fanaticism promoted futile squabbling within the Social Democratic movement as a whole and specifically among the Bolsheviks, absorbing much of their energy in ways that were quite irrelevant to the concerns of the workers in Russia. Moreover, the factional skulduggery that Lenin practiced rendered him vulnerable to manipulation by the tsar's police, who could readily plant their agents in the organization of a leader who was desperate for loyal "supporters." Ironically, both the police and Lenin favored the factional splintering of the revolutionary movement, and in the long run the question is which side was the gainer.

While Shukman finds the revolutionary leadership beset with difficulties, S. S. Oldenburg maintains that the Russian social and economic system was gaining strength and stability on the eve of the World War. His cardinal point is that the Russia of 1914 was very different from the Russia of 1905. Partly through firm government leadership, partly through independent efforts among the populace, Russia had advanced rapidly on the path to modernization. Many elements in his case—educational progress, economic growth, social transformation— would be present in almost any version of the optimistic view of the Russian empire on the eve of World War I. What is more unusual is Oldenburg's opinion that the political basis of successful modernization could only be traditional monarchy. Whether or not one agrees with him, it is worth considering the possibility that parliamentary democracy and authoritarian socialism are not the only possible forms of government in a country that is rapidly modernizing its economy, social structure, and culture. The shortcomings of the government of Nicholas II have been well advertised and the lurid presence of Rasputin in the imperial court has been dramatized, with the implication that one could hardly expect such a government to survive. In reality Rasputin did not play a significant role in public affairs before World War I. The regime did have some reserves in its fight for survival. Yaney's discussion of the agrarian reforms suggests that one should not dismiss lightly Oldenburg's high regard for the civil service. Moreover, liberal historians have tended to pay little attention to the harsher aspects of the situation: the tsar's political police had thoroughly penetrated the radical parties with its agents by 1914, and the army was both large and loyal. It is open to question whether any violent uprising against the tsar could have succeeded before the decimation of the regular officer corps and enlisted personnel in the slaughter of World War I.

Oldenburg's case does not rest wholly on the strength of the government. The impressive rise in mass education on all levels was not, he recognizes, completely the work of the government. This is a vital factor to be reckoned with in appraising the condition of Russia at this time, and there is no doubt that a great advance in this field had occurred since 1905. Did this advance in education signify the enlargement of the radical intelligentsia (a risk that Oldenburg recognizes), or the foundation of a modernized, relatively democratic social order (as he prefers to think)? Another major development that Oldenburg sketches, which was largely independent of the government, was the cooperative movement. It may be, however, that his treatment of this movement does not make clear that in agriculture some marketing cooperatives made great strides, along with consumer and credit cooperatives.

In the last selection Hans Rogger reconsiders the whole problem from the political, social, and cultural points of view. While he does not attempt to minimize the seriousness of the problems facing Russia, he is too aware of the complexity of the crosscurrents in Russian life in 1914 to accept a definite conclusion that the country was on the brink of disintegration, war or no war. The essay suggests that the historian must resist the temptation to build the strongest possible case for the thesis that attracts him, by selecting mainly or only evidence that will support the thesis. Rogger calls attention to contradictory tendencies, which make any unqualified conclusion questionable. His closing intimation that further research along some lines is needed may owe something to his own specialized research on the "radicals of the Right" in Russia after 1905. Even though these Right extremists never came close to playing a dominant role, the history of some other European countries certainly suggests that authoritarian, non-Communist regimes can succeed in ruling a modern country.

This is to suggest that the student of this period in Russian history should be open-minded concerning the alternative models, both of evolution and of revolution, which may be applicable. The experience of the twentieth century does not confirm the expectations of either of the great nineteenth-century doctrines of progress: liberalism or Marxism. We have witnessed neither an advance of man through enlightened self-interest to a world of parliamentary, capitalistic democra-

cies, nor the revolutionary replacement of this kind of society in all the economically advanced countries by a proletarian upheaval leading to the withering away
of the state under socialism.

Yet these classical models of development still dominate much of the thinking
about modern history, and a majority of the historians whose writings appear in
this book accept one or the other. One of the assumptions of this book is that Soviet
historical writing deserves a serious reading in spite of its ideological cant, and, by
the same token, such writers as Miliukov and Pares are not to be summarily
dismissed because of their antique liberal preconceptions. What I am suggesting is
that a critical reading of all these historians of Russia, and, if possible, of some of
the writers who have recently taken up the general problem of modernization, may
help the reader to reach an appraisal of the situation in Russia from 1905 to 1914
which comes closer than the old, ideologically based interpretations to doing justice
to the history of this great country in our turbulent century.[1]

---

[1]Recent investigations of the general problem of modernization include Cyril E. Black, *The Dynamics of
Modernization* (New York, 1966), Barrington Moore, Jr., *The Peasant Origins of Totalitarianism and Democracy*
(Boston, 1966), and Theodore H. Von Laue, *The Global City. Freedom, Power, and Necessity in the Age of
World Revolutions* (Philadelphia, 1969).

Material appearing in square brackets in the following selections is inserted by the editor of the
present book.

In the reprinted selections footnotes appearing in the original sources have in general been omitted
unless they contribute to the argument or better understanding of the selection.

Dates are given in the "old style" (Julian calendar), which was in use in Russia before 1918. The
corresponding dates in the Gregorian calendar, which was in use in the West, are thirteen days later.

No evaluation of the Revolution of 1905 can overlook the soviets (councils) of workers' deputies that appeared in the fall of the year. Although they did not last long in 1905, they provided a genuinely popular myth, which was finally captured by Lenin's Bolshevik party in 1917. The only substantial study of this subject outside the Soviet Union is *Die Rätbewegung in Russland 1905–1921* by OSKAR ANWEILER (b. 1925), a professor at the Ruhr–Universität Bochum in West Germany. Anweiler is also author of the most extensive history in any language of schools and education in Soviet Russia. While he assigns great importance to the industrial workers as a revolutionary force, his interpretation of the struggle in Russia is essentially pluralistic, stressing the interaction of diverse political and social elements. This sets it apart from the monist Soviet approach in the second selection.*

Oskar Anweiler

The Opening of New Possibilities

The year 1917 is a decisive turning point in modern Russian history. So undisputed and generally acknowledged is this fact, that we must avoid the danger of treating one-sidedly all the events preceding the October Revolution, considering them as "precursors" of 1917. This viewpoint, which all Soviet historiography assumes, also provides the framework for the interpretation of the first Russian Revolution of 1905. Lenin's phrase, "the dress rehearsal" of 1905, which was followed by the "performance" in 1917, forms the starting point and main theme of Soviet presentations of 1905, and this conception has been widely accepted in non-Soviet research as well. According to this view, the Revolution of 1905 represents only one step (albeit significant) in the *predetermined* course of Russian history, of which the Revolution of 1917 and the Bolsheviks' seizure of power is the conclusion. In opposition to this view the present essay asks that the reader consider the Revolution of 1905 as a historical phenomenon *in its own right* and not in the light of the final outcome in 1917. The strands that connect the two events, and which deserve our attention in their own right, must be considered as part of the course of events, not as preconceptions imposed from outside. If one examines the Revolution of 1905 in this way,

---

*From Oskar Anweiler, "Die russische Revolution von 1905. Aus Anlass ihres 50. Jahrestages" ("The Russian Revolution of 1905. On the Occasion of Its Fiftieth Anniversary"), *Jahrbücher für Geschichte Osteuropas,* N. F. 3, 1955, pp. 161–176. By permission. Translated by Robert H. McNeal.

it is the present writer's belief that it will be seen to deserve a place as a *turning point* in Russian history. . . .

The growing revolutionary crisis that was threatening at the opening of the twentieth century was sharpened and its outbreak hastened by the unsuccessful course of the Russo-Japanese War. In the upper economic strata there was ever stronger criticism of the inadequate military performance, for which the bureaucracy was, for the most part, blamed. The liberal opposition organized a campaign of meetings and petitions, which reached its peak in a congress of over one hundred zemstvo [local self-government] representatives from 32 provinces, which met in Petersburg in November 1904. The climax of the reform movement was an appeal for a constituent assembly. There was also a renewed upsurge of the workers' strike movement at the end of 1904 as a result of rising prices.

But the onset of the revolution came from another quarter, which no one had anticipated. In early April 1904, the young priest Georgii Gapon, with the concurrence of the authorities, founded in Petersburg a union for the cultural and social welfare of the metal workers, and at the same time for their patriotic indoctrination. These efforts of some circles in the regime to use stooges to draw the workers away from the influence of the revolutionaries was known as *"zubatovshchina"* [after the police officer Zubatov, who first developed this tactic], or "police socialism." It was a murky mixture of Gapon's idealistic zeal, police tactics, and the naïve hopes of the masses. Gapon had connections with some former Social Democratic workers who wished to transform the new organization into a fighting band of the workers' elite. Under the influence of the liberals' petition campaign, the leadership of the Gapon organization took up the idea of presenting a workers' petition to the tsar. Together with some left liberals Gapon composed a petition, which was circulated among the workers in early January 1905. . . .

The outcome of the procession to the Winter Palace [to present the petition to the tsar] on Sunday, January 9, involving about 100,000 persons, is well known. Completely misjudging the psychology of the working masses that came to the tsar's palace, the regime did the most fatal thing possible: the brutal fusillade of the soldiers destroyed the faith of the workers in the tsar. Contrary to the wishes of the participants, "Bloody Sunday" began the Russian revolution. That this was the beginning of the revolution shows clearly that it was not a question of accidental and isolated despair, but a partial manifestation of a general fermentation process that had already taken hold of a broad economic stratum and reached the exploding point among the Petersburg workers.

One may characterize the time from January until the summer of 1905 as the period in which the revolution spread out from its source in Petersburg. It appears as a confused interaction of different political and social tendencies and individual acts, ranging from the petition and deputation campaign of the liberals to the strikes and demonstrations of the workers, to peasant uprisings and sailors' mutinies. The conflict of class interests, which reached various levels of political consciousness, depending on the degree to which a given group was organized, prevented the establishment of a united front against tsarism. In the following, we will restrict ourselves to identification of the characteristics of the events.

1. Immediately after January 9, there were major *workers' strikes* and demonstra-

tions in all the major cities of the Russian Empire. The number of strikers in Moscow in January and February 1905 was higher than in the preceding ten years combined. The non-Russian peoples of the borderlands (Poles, Balts, Caucasians) played a leading role, and the movement thus assumed a much sharper political character. On the other hand, the strike movement among the Great Russians, until October 1905, was predominantly economic in motivation and developed political goals only gradually. The main reasons for this were: (a) The oppressive social condition of the Russian worker impelled him to strive for an immediate improvement of his working and living conditions before becoming concerned with a political struggle against the regime. (b) Along with the mainstream of metal and textile workers, who already could look back on ten years of strike action, there were now added new strata, semiproletarian in character (bakers, stevedores, city transport workers, merchants' employees, etc.), which advanced social demands for the first time. (c) Despite the awakening of a broader mass of the populace, the revolutionary organizations were still not in a position to conduct their agitational and propagandistic work on a large scale.

In May 1905 the strike movement reached a new high point. The defeat of the Russian fleet at Tsushima on May 14 raised the temperature of the domestic political atmosphere and weakened the power of the regime. Often the workers gained permission from the local authorities to hold their meetings. The material result of the strike movement was mainly the reduction of the working day to ten, nine and sometimes eight hours. The main centers of strike activity were Ivanovo Voznesensk and Kostroma in the Moscow industrial region and Lodz in Poland.

The workers' strike movement provided the dynamic force of the first Russian revolution. This fact points up the unique character of the Revolution of 1905: the youngest economic stratum, the industrial proletariat, advanced its claims, while older problems (the agrarian and constitutional questions) still awaited solution. The weakness of the numbers and consciousness of the Russian bourgeoisie and the inadequate revolutionary organization of the peasantry made the workers the leading fighters in the "bourgeois revolution," which in western Europe had been carried out by the bourgeoisie itself. The Russian worker joined battle for his social advancement not only with the entrepreneurs and the power of capital, but also with the police and the power of tsarism. The development of the workers' movement in 1905 clearly shows that the workers were on the whole inclined to political solutions because they understood that effective social reform without political changes was impossible in the Russian Empire. Finally, in the political general strike of October the proletariat became the principal fighting force of all the oppositional strata of the populace. The workers therefore stood at the summit of the Russian revolutionary movement.

2. The Revolution of 1905 began with the workers' petition-march to the tsar, but the idea of a petition was a result of the earlier liberal campaign in the spring of 1904. Now the events of Bloody Sunday stimulated the liberal opposition movement. In numerous protest meetings the intelligentsia condemned the action of the regime against the Petersburg workers. During January and February the universities and other institutions of higher education had to be closed because the students were using the buildings for antigovernment demonstrations. The previously existing associations of the liberal pro-

fessions [called unions although they were not labor unions in the usual sense] formed the basis for the professional-political organization of the Russian intelligentsia. At the beginning of May the individual unions joined in an all-Russian "Union of Unions," which adopted a still more radical position.

The other wing of the liberal movement, the zemstvo opposition, in March 1905 began holding congresses of delegates, inviting representatives of the city dumas [elected councils] in May. Under the influence of military defeats in the Far East and the growing domestic ferment, these congresses moved more and more toward the left, without, however, departing from the principle of constitutional monarchy and calling for a republic. . . .

Liberal hopes for concessions from the tsar and the regime could be traced to their fear of the danger of a radical social revolution and the breakup of the multinational empire. In an imploring appeal to Nicholas II on June 6, a delegation asked the tsar for confidence in the "healthy forces" of the country and for the guarantee of freedom and a constitution. When the regime remained deaf to the liberals' appeals for reform, the latter decided to "go to the people." At the July congress [of zemstvo delegates, the liberal] Petrunkevich said,

Until now we have hoped for a reform from above, but now the people are our only hope. . . . The ineptitude and impotence of the regime has brought on the revolution. . . . Our duty is to devote all our efforts to avoiding bloodshed. We cannot stop the storm, but we must in any case take care that a strong shock is avoided.

The efforts of the liberals to win broad mass support for their program were complicated by the sense of deep alienation of the peasants and workers from the ideals of formal democracy and parliamentarianism on the Western model, which the liberal intelligentsia represented. Concrete economic questions and not the problem of constitutional law held first priority in their interests. Nevertheless, the goal of a constituent assembly, which possessed symbolic powers of attraction for the masses, shone bright enough to bring the liberals a majority in the First Duma. As the experience of 1917 later showed, the only hope for survival of the monarchy and also for avoidance of a total revolution lay in the timely adaptation of tsarism to the moderate program of the Russian liberals.

3. The unrest among the peasants, sailors, and soldiers came as a result of the general revolutionization of the country rather than as a direct consequence of the January events. A series of spontaneous *peasant revolts* broke out in the spring and fall of 1905 and reached their peak in the summer of 1906. The leading outbreaks were in Latvia and Georgia and in the Great Russian provinces of Tver, Samarra, and Saratov. The form of the agrarian movement varied locally: destruction of farm buildings, seizure of cattle and grain, cutting down wood lots, arbitrary occupation of landlords' land. The peasant "strike" was also widespread: the peasants refused to pay rent, perform certain services, etc., until their demands were satisfied. The people who spread revolutionary ideas among the peasants—especially the "third element" of the zemstvo (teachers, doctors, veterinarians, agronomists, and others who were employed by the zemstvo) and the individual agitators who came from the city—had to adapt themselves to the practical needs of the peasantry. Direct political agitation among the peasants against the tsar brought only meager results. Nevertheless, the mass of the peasantry, which was in ferment and ready to explode, was a powerful reserve force, which the revolution sought to

utilize, just as the regime tried to build upon the ignorance and traditional conservatism of the peasantry. The idea of a people's uprising, of which the narodniks [Russian socialists of the 1870s] had dreamed, appeared again on the horizon of the revolutionary in 1905 and 1906. These dreams were not fulfilled, because the numerous local revolts were not coordinated with one another or with the movement in the cities.

4. In 1905 and 1906 mutinies in the armed forces, even more than the peasant uprisings, arose from accidental causes and not from any clear political intent. Bad food and clothing, callous officers, cancellation of leave, harsh treatment of reservists (especially in the Manchurian army) [the Russian force in the Far East] led to elemental unrest in individual army units, which, however, was suppressed by loyal detachments comparatively easily. Nevertheless, there were moments in the course of the revolution when the soldiers' and sailors' movement went beyond isolated, individual actions, especially the mutiny on the battleship *Potemkin* in May 1905 and the unrest among the soldiers which accompanied the Moscow uprising of December 1905. In both cases the mutineers failed to establish cooperation with the concurrent workers' movements, in Odessa and Moscow respectively. Similarly, the soldiers of the Manchurian army, which in November or December 1905 controlled the Trans-Siberian Railroad, finally had to yield to a punitive expedition. The struggle for control of the armed forces, which the revolutionaries waged in 1905, was successful only in a few cases. Trotsky's sharp but pertinent judgment is valid for the attitude of the Russian army as a whole: "On the politically blunted mind of the *muzhik* [peasant]—who in his own village sets fire to the *barin's* [land-lord's] buildings, but who shoots the workers when dressed in a soldier's tunic—the first wave of the Russian revolution was shattered."

5. The revolutionary unrest of 1905 would never have reached this extent if there had been at the head of the state a resolute, politically clear-thinking monarch who grasped the situation and was advised by men of the same caliber. Instead, there was the mediocre tsar Nicholas II, surrounded by equally average advisers, who lacked any large conception of the future. The regime undermined its own authority through a mixture of halfway concessions and strong measures. At the end of this vacillating policy stood the preliminary capitulation of tsarism to the revolution in October 1905.

Immediately following Bloody Sunday in Petersburg, the regime established two commissions to study the labor question. One of these, under Senator Shidlovsky, even was to include elected workers. With the radicalization of the Petersburg workers, the election assumed the character of a political demonstration, and the commission was disbanded before it met. This was the only attempt of the regime in 1905 to approach the solution of the labor question in a legal way.

On February 18 the tsar issued a highly significant rescript to the newly appointed minister of internal affairs, Bulygin. This was an order to prepare a plan for a consultative legislative assembly—an imperial duma. After many months of preparation and discussion, reaching its final stage in the narrow circle of the tsar's confidants at Peterhof Palace, the so-called Bulygin Duma plan legally came into effect on August 6, 1905. In the time that had passed, however, the internal political situation had changed so much that the concessions, which in the eyes of the tsar were far-reaching, were rejected as inadequate by public opinion, that is, by the moderate liberals. . . .

But it appeared in the late summer of 1905, in contrast to the stormy developments of the first half of the year, that a stabilization of the domestic situation was developing in Russia. The conclusion of peace with Japan on August 23 (September 5 in the Western calendar) freed the rear of the regime, so that it could combat domestic unrest energetically. Through limited concessions on the constitutional question, certain improvements in the status of non-Orthodox Christians and Jews, the granting of autonomy to the universities, as well as renewed deliberations on an agrarian reform, the Petersburg government hoped to forestall the revolutionary tendency in society and to conserve the old governmental order essentially unchanged. Within a few weeks, however, this hope proved illusory.

The high point of the Revolution of 1905 was marked by two events: the October strike and the December uprising. Between the two lay the "Days of Freedom," a time of high revolutionary tension throughout the country, awakening unrest on one side and indecisive official policies on the other. In these days a new public political life took shape in Russia, still passionately agitated and oscillating between extremes. The end of these two brief months of the high tide of revolution was marked by the military victory of the old order and its about-face in the direction of reaction. The political product of the revolution was the October Manifesto, a document that represented the preliminary capitulation of tsarism to the revolution and which from the start was burdened with the political dishonesty with which it was issued. No renewal of Russia could come on this basis, only the abortive constitutional experiment of the first two Dumas.

1. The strike movement, which had subsided considerably in the summer, flared up anew in the second half of September with a strike of Moscow printing workers. In a few days it quickly spread to other Moscow factories. Beginning on September 24 a series of bloody encounters with police and Cossacks aroused the masses, and on the 27th a general strike began. After several days the movement seemed to be petering out, but the spark leaped to Petersburg, where on October 3 the printers began a sympathy strike. This wave, too, was receding when on October 6 the workers of the Kazan railroad shops in Moscow walked out. . . .

This was the real root of the October strike. In a few days the railroad strike spread to all the lines in Russia. As early as the 13th it included all lines except those in Finland, and by the 16th they too stopped. Beginning on October 10 the strike included factory workers, and after the 12th it became a general strike, embracing both private and public employees, professional people, and the postal-telegraph-telephone services. Moscow and Petersburg led the way; all the major cities followed; and a series of small ones were also drawn into the wave of strikes.

The principal characteristic of the great October strike was that it was political from the first day. In a moment the struggle of the railroad workers' congress for the inviolability of the individual became a struggle for personal and bourgeois freedom in general, for a constitution, a political amnesty, and so on. The predominant slogan called for a constituent assembly based on a general, equal, direct, and secret election.

Through the participation of nonproletarian elements, the October strike as-

sumed the character of a political demonstration of *all* oppositional social groups
against the tsarist system. The founding
congress of the Constitutional Democrats,
which met in Petersburg at this time (October 12–18), declared its solidarity with
the strikers and likewise called for the convocation of a national assembly. The
Union of Unions took an active part in the
organization of the strike among salaried
employees and professional people. Numerous employers permitted workers to
hold meetings in the factories, paid them
in full or part for the days they were on
strike, and did not fire any individual
workers for participating in the strike. The
city dumas either sympathized with the
strike movement or at least maintained
neutrality. They gave financial support to
the strikers, accepted workers' representatives at their meetings, and petitioned the
authorities and the military to withdraw.

After October 14 the capital of the Russian Empire was without railroad communications, city transportation, lighting, tele-
phones, newspapers, and in part without
operating business firms. The tsar and his
family were at Peterhof [not far outside the
city along the coast] and the ministers
could reach them [from Petersburg] only
by means of the imperial yacht. In the face
of this desperate situation and the reports
of catastrophe that were pouring in from
all over Russia, the tsar sought the help of
Witte, whose prestige was high again after
the peace treaty [which he had negotiated]
with Japan, appointing him chairman of
the council of ministers. . . .

Witte saw that the only way to avoid a
revolution was "to place the state at the
head of the liberation movement." With
his ideas of "reform from above" he stood
almost alone in the cabinet. Since nobody
in the tsar's entourage had any better ad-
vice, or was willing to assume the post of
military dictator, the tsar was persuaded to

sign a manifesto to the people of Russia
that Witte had composed. On October 17
the document, henceforth known as the
"October Manifesto," was published and
dispatched by telegraph to even the most
remote parts of the empire.

The October Manifesto granted bourgeois civil liberty, broadened the franchise
for the elections to the Duma to include
previously excluded groups [especially factory workers], and gave the Duma the power to pass laws, as contrasted with merely
advisory functions. In the eyes of the majority of the Russian people this signified
nothing other than the end of the old autocracy and the beginning of a parliamen-
tary-constitutional era. The masses reacted
to the manifesto in this spirit. After October 19 the railroads began operation
again; the united front of the opposition
began to disintegrate. Only the revolutionary leaders and a narrow stratum of the
politically advanced workers maintained
their mistrust of the regime and called for
a broader struggle. Today we can confirm
what the radicals were already saying at
the time: that Nicholas II never sincerely
considered permitting a basic change in
the Russian form of government, breaking
the vow he had made at his father's
deathbed to maintain the integrity of the
autocracy. Witte did indeed want to base
his policy on the October Manifesto, but it
soon became evident that his sphere of authority was limited. Two known conservatives, Trepov and Durnovo, retained their
influential posts as palace commander and
minister of internal affairs respectively,
and carried on reactionary intrigues behind Witte's back.

Another event revealed still more drasti-
cally the inner contradictions in the revo-
lution-wracked land. The wave of
pogroms, which erupted mainly in the
cities of the Jewish Pale of Settlement in
the west and southwest [the only areas in

the empire in which most Jews were permitted to live], unleashed by the "Black Hundreds" [violent Russian nationalist organizations] and frequently condoned by the authorities, was the response of the mass instinct of the politically backward part of the population to the apparent victory of the revolution. It also revealed the danger of civil war, which both the extreme Right and the extreme Left called for. The October Manifesto was not the end of the revolution but the signal for a broader struggle.

2. The period between the proclamation of the October Manifesto and the Moscow uprising of December—the "Days of Freedom" as they are called in Russian revolutionary literature—is characterized by an equilibrium, a balance of power between the state and the revolution. "The autocracy *already* lacked the power to move openly against the revolution. The revolution *still* lacked the power to deal the decisive blow to the enemy. This fluctuation of its power, almost maintaining a balance [between the state and its enemies], inevitably breeds panic and brings about the transition from repression to concession," wrote Lenin in this period. As a result, Russia had no stable government for nearly two months; the domestic turmoil increased rather than diminished; and a "complete" victory of the revolution seemed quite possible. The regime failed to take legislative measures to guarantee the freedoms promised by the October Manifesto, which would have removed the political struggle from the street, in the form of revolutionary clashes, to the parliamentary arena. Thus tsarism forced the groups of the populace who were not satisfied with paper concessions to try to seize freedom with their own hands, intensifying the political struggle. . . .

After a brief interval the strike movement expanded. In contrast with the essentially economic strikes of the period before October, the political demonstration-strike was now dominant. For example, in early November the Petersburg Soviet organized a strike in sympathy with the Polish movement for national autonomy and with the Kronstadt sailors who had mutinied and been condemned by a court martial. The struggle for an eight-hour day in Petersburg revealed the social essence of the workers' revolution. The spontaneous movement for the introduction of the eight-hour day in the factories, which the labor leaders had accepted only reluctantly, ended in failure. The result was a far-reaching antagonism within the united front of the October days, which inaugurated a turn to the right on the part of the bourgeoisie.

At the peak of the October strike the liberals, in Miliukov's words, "stood on the left wing of the Russian political movement," and the dividing line between them and the right was more sharply drawn than between the liberals and the left. From the viewpoint of the tsar and the conservatives the Kadets seemed to be at least as dangerous as the socialists, possessing the most talented leaders, big newspapers, and substantial financial resources. After the proclamation of the October Manifesto, Witte attempted to hold talks with the Kadets concerning their participation in the cabinet. However, the negotiations broke down over the person of Durnovo, who was unacceptable to the liberals, but still more because the Kadets had to take account of the revolutionary mood of the country.

After the proclamation of the October Manifesto a differentiation of parties appeared within the liberal-bourgeois opposition. The right zemstvo-opposition and industrial-commercial circles, which had advanced only moderate political demands, saw their wishes fulfilled in the promises of the Manifesto. They formed the "Union of October 17" ("Octobrists"), which renounced the demand for a constituent assembly and promised their support to Witte's cabinet. The left majority of the zemstvo movement and the liberal intelligentsia, which formed the Kadet party, upheld the call for a constituent assembly, but wished to attain this through the Duma and not by means of a bloody revolution. In the course of November and December the specter of the "Red Revolution" increasingly concerned the liberals and influenced their attitude toward the regime, of which they demanded energetic action. The liberals and socialists were now divided concerning their goals: a constitutional monarchy in collaboration with the tsar or a democratic republic resulting from a popular revolution. . . .

The tsarist regime experienced its most dangerous crisis at the end of November and beginning of December. Faced with the danger of an elemental upheaval, the regime determined to seize the initiative once more and wage a resolute struggle against the revolution. This led the Revolution of 1905 to its bloody high point, which was at the same time its turning point.

3. The conflict was started by the arrest of the Petersburg soviet on December 3. On the previous day a decree had appeared forbidding strikes of railroad, postal, telegraph and telephone services, on pain of severe punishment, which hindered the outbreak of the expected wave of strikes following the arrest of the soviet. In Petersburg the general strike called by the replacements for the arrested soviet did not in fact achieve the breadth and intensity of the earlier strike. The critical point of the revolutionary movement moved to Moscow, where a general strike started on December 7 and was transformed into an armed uprising [which was crushed in heavy fighting]. . . .

The Moscow uprising was the only case during the revolution in which tsarism faced a substantial opponent on the field of battle. The numerous strikes that broke out in the provinces as echoes of the events in the capitals and the single small uprising in the Donets region remained isolated. After mid-December the regime dispatched numerous punitive military expeditions to the restive areas, especially the Baltic, Caucasus, and Siberia. These rigorous measures re-established the authority of the government. Thus the events of December represented "a decisive turn of Russian domestic politics toward the most extreme reaction" [Lenin].

For the historian looking back, this is the decisive turning point, but for the contemporary it remained an open question at the beginning of the year 1906 whether a renewed upsurge of revolution was at hand. . . .

Sometimes an author speaks with enhanced authority if he remains anonymous. This probably explains why the essay on the fiftieth anniversary of the Russian Revolution of 1905–1907 that appeared in HISTORICAL TRANSACTIONS *(Istoricheskie Zapiski)* was unsigned. The object of the exercise was to reaffirm with the weightiest ideological authority that the main lines of the approved interpretation of the revolution remained unchanged, even though the cult of Stalin had gone into decline shortly after his death in 1953, his name being markedly absent from the anniversary essay. Since the year of the fiftieth anniversary, no basic change in this interpretation has appeared, although nationalist rhetoric has been tempered in most Soviet writing. Although the style of this essay is likely to alienate a good many readers, it is worthwhile to seek the fundamental points in this interpretation and to consider the extent to which they may be acceptable to a non-Leninist.*

Historical Transactions:
Dress Rehearsal for 1917

The fiftieth anniversary of the bourgeois-democratic revolution of 1905–1907 is an important date in the life of our country and of the whole international revolutionary movement.

The bourgeois-democratic revolution of 1905–1907 is one of the brightest pages in the history of our Motherland. This was an authentic people's revolution in which the working class and peasantry, that is, the overwhelming majority of the country, waged a heroic struggle against autocracy. The first Russian revolution played a great historic role in the preparation of the Great October Socialist Revolution. It served and serves as an inspiring example and an inexhaustible source of experience in battle for the international proletariat in the fulfillment of its tasks of liberation.

The greatest world-wide historical significance of the Revolution of 1905–1907 is that it ended a period of "the most tranquil and peaceful development of capitalism" [Lenin] and opened a period of the greatest shocks and storms, which marked the beginning of the most profound crisis of the world capitalist system. The first Russian revolution enriched Marxism with new historical experience, played a tremendous role in the further development of

*From *Piatidesiatiletie russkoi revoliutsii 1905-1907 gg.—pervoi narodnoi revoliutsii epokhi imperializma* ("The Fiftieth Anniversary of the Russian Revolution of 1905-1907—The First People's Revolution of the Epoch of Imperialism"), *Istoricheskie Zapiski (Historical Transactions)*, vol. 49, pp. 3–9. Translated by Robert H. McNeal.

the ideology and policy of Leninism, which represented a new stage in the creative development of Marxist theory. The Revolution of 1905–1907 clearly demonstrated that the center of the world revolutionary movement had been transferred to Russia. In this connection, the study of the history of the first Russian revolution, its experience, its specific features, which sharply distinguish it from the previous bourgeois-democratic revolutions in the West, has not only scholarly but also political significance.

The enormous significance of the first Russian revolution stems from the objective conditions that existed in the country at the beginning of the twentieth century and from the place that Russia occupied in the system of international imperialism. Pursuing the goal of the overthrow of tsarism, the establishment of a democratic republic, the introduction of an eight-hour day, and the confiscation of the landlords' land, the Revolution of 1905–1907 was bourgeois-democratic in its character and tasks. In this it resembled the bourgeois-democratic revolutions in the West. But the fundamentally different historical conditions on which the revolution was based evoked a series of basically new characteristics which distinguished it from previous revolutions and immeasurably enhanced its role and significance for the subsequent fate of Russia, as well as the fate of all humanity.

In this connection it was of decisive importance that the first Russian revolution occurred in the period of imperialism. In contrast to premonopoly capitalism, which was still in its ascending phase, imperialism represented dying capitalism. It carried to their limits the antagonistic contradictions that are peculiar to capitalist production and placed on the order of the day the question of social revolution, the destruction of the old, outworn rela-

tions of production and their replacement by new, socialist relations of production.

At the beginning of the revolution, capitalism in Russia had already entered the imperialist stage of its development, with all its characteristic parasitism and decay. On the other hand, there were special features of the economic and political situation in Russia in this period: the presence of very potent remnants of serfdom in the economy of the country (most of all in landholding) and the political domination of the landlords, which strengthened and deepened the contradictions of imperialism. . . .

It followed from the specific features of the Russian revolution in the period of imperialism that the victory of the bourgeois revolution in Russia could not be the victory of the bourgeoisie. Economically and politically bound by a multitude of ties with tsardom and the landlords, the liberal bourgeoisie was a counterrevolutionary force that tried to gain control of the revolutionary movement in order to limit it, to keep the revolution from following through to its conclusion, to interrupt it by making a deal with the autocracy over the heads of the people.

The victory of the bourgeois revolution in Russia was possible only as the victory of the working class and peasantry, as the victory of the revolutionary-democratic dictatorship of the proletariat and peasantry. The proletariat, as the only consistent spokesman for the basic interests of the overwhelming majority of the nation, formed the vanguard and leading force of the revolution. It was vitally interested in the complete victory of the democratic revolution. Following the liquidation of the feudal remnants, such a victory would have given the proletariat a chance to organize itself better, to accumulate experience in the political leadership of the working masses. It would have created favorable conditions for the struggle for socialism.

The revolution confirmed the well-known Leninist proposition that the strength of the proletariat is incomparably greater than its share of the population of a country. Never before in world history has the specifically proletarian means of struggle, the strike, played such an enormous role, as in the first Russian revolution. The number of striking workers in 1905 reached three million (and with the railroad and postal-telegraph employees [including white-collar staff], four million). In the following year of the revolution the strike movement also was very great, although diminishing. There were one million strikers in 1906; in 1907 there were 750,000. It was quite characteristic that the major industrial centers provided the largest number of strikers, and the larger the factory, the more often it struck and the more tenaciously it maintained its strikes. The most skilled and politically conscious stratum of the working class — the metal industry workers, followed by the textile workers — formed the vanguard of the strike movement. In the article "On Strike Statistics in Russia," V. I. Lenin stated that the minimum number of strikers in Russia in 1905–1907 "exceeded the maximum ever achieved in the most capitalistic country in the world." The strike movement assumed vast proportions thanks to the intermixture of economic and political strikes.

The Revolution of 1905–1907 decided in practice the argument between the Bolsheviks and opportunists concerning the role of mass political strikes in the revolution. As is known, the opportunist leaders of west European social democracy called the general strike "general nonsense." The first Russian revolution convincingly showed that the mass strike is a powerful weapon in the hands of the proletariat in its political struggle and a necessary precursor to the highest form of revolutionary struggle—armed uprising. For the first time in history the political strike was transformed into a means of general popular struggle for freedom. This was a result of the peculiar feature of the bourgeois-democratic revolution of 1905–1907: It was a revolution of the proletariat in its forms and means of struggle, by the decisive impact of the proletariat on the whole course of events.

Inasmuch as the main remnant of serfdom was the retention of landlord landholding, the agrarian, peasant question was a central one for the Russian bourgeois-democratic revolution.

The natural ally of the proletariat in the revolution was the entire peasantry, which was interested in getting landlord, church, and state lands and in winning democratic freedom.

The Russian working class exercised great influence on the peasantry, arousing it to revolutionary struggle. Despite its vacillations, the Russian peasantry was at this time more revolutionary, more developed, more advanced than the peasantry of the West in the period of bourgeois revolutions. V. I. Lenin wrote: "In the first period of the Russian revolution our peasants created an agrarian movement that was incomparably stronger, surer, politically more conscious than in the previous bourgeois revolutions of the nineteenth century." The working class imbued the peasantry with this consciousness, organization, steadfastness. The common struggle of the proletariat and peasantry against tsarism, landlords, and capitalists stemmed from their common, fundamental economic and political interest, their mutual interest in the economic and social-political progress of the country. . . .

Russia was unusual in being a multinational state in which over half the population consisted of non-Russian nationalities. This huge mass of the non-Russian population was subjected by tsarism to even worse conditions of existence than the Russian workers and peasants. When Russia entered the period of imperialism, national oppression also was intensified. Clearly the national question in Russia was of no small significance. Therefore, the proletariat had to assume the leadership of not only the peasant movement but also the growing national-liberation struggle of the peoples of the borderlands of Russia. Led by the Bolshevik party, the proletariat was able to combine the interests of the proletarian liberation movement as a whole with the specific national interests of the oppressed peoples of Russia. The policy of the proletariat promoted the drawing together of peoples, of their internationalist education; it promoted the growth of trust in the Russian people. Relying on the support of the workers of the [non-Russian] national regions, the Russian working class waged a successful struggle against the local national bourgeoisie for the leadership of the national liberation movement. The working class held the advantage in this struggle because it was a consistent opponent of all kinds of oppression, all variants of the landlord-capitalist order, and not only national oppression. Thus the working class secured the support of the multimillions of the toiling masses of the non-Russian peoples.

The proletariat of the largest industrial centers of the national regions of Russia— Baku, Lodz, Warsaw, Riga, Reval, and other places — stood in the front ranks of the revolutionary fighters for the overthrow of tsarism. In Latvia the peasants threatened the holdings of the German barons and waged a stubborn struggle against the armed detachments of the landlords and regular tsarist troops. The oppressed peoples of the Caucasus, Central Asia, the Volga area, and Siberia rose in struggle against tsarism. The peasant movement in Georgia attained unprecedented scope. Thus the conditions of the revolution formed a united front of toilers of multinational Russia under the leadership of the Russian working class.

Revolution, V. I. Lenin said more than once, is civil war. The proletariat cannot win this war if it has not formed its revolutionary army. The Bolshevik party attached great importance to the arming of the people, the questions of military organization, the formation of combat teams, the preparation and acquisition of arms, the winning of soldiers and sailors to the side of the revolution.

The entire course of the revolution inevitably drew the masses toward the highest form of struggle — the armed uprising. The December armed uprising [in Moscow] was the culminating point in the first Russian revolution. It was the natural completion of the preceding mass struggle. As V. I. Lenin stated, even the statistical data on the number of participants in purely political strikes testifies to this: 123,000 in January 1905; 328,000 in October; but in December, 372,000. The grandiose political strike of the workers, combined with armed mutinies of sailors at Kronstadt and Sevastopol, the disturbances and armed demonstrations in military units, and mass peasant uprisings made the transition to armed uprising completely unavoidable. . . .

By its revolutionary struggle the proletariat united all the revolutionary forces of the country. And after its defeat the proletariat did not allow the banner of revolution to slip from its hands. It continued to call for a new armed struggle, to educate, to unite, to organize the forces for this struggle. In December 1905 the people received its baptism of fire. It was no longer its former self. It had been tempered, reborn and had brought forth from its midst the army of warriors that was victorious in 1917.

The experience of the armed uprising in December 1905 had enormous significance for the further struggle of the working class of Russia. In effect the December armed uprising of the revolutionary masses had started to overthrow the old order and thereby demonstrated the possibility of setting up the democratic republic. . . .

The soviets of workers' deputies, which were formed on the initiative of the revolutionary proletariat in many industrial centers, were organs of the armed uprising. On the initiative of the revolutionary masses, soviets of soldiers' deputies and soviets of peasants' deputies were also formed. The soviets were at the same time organs of the new order that was being born. In the years of the first Russian revolution the Bolsheviks already regarded the soviets as the state-form of the revolutionary-democratic dictatorship of workers and peasants, while the Mensheviks looked on them as organs of local self-government. The appearance of the soviets as the embryonic organs of the new state apparatus was objective proof that in the period of imperialism the general democratic revolution could not in the course of things stop at the first stage, but could and should continue on to the succeeding, socialist stage. For the main feature of the socialist revolution, which distinguishes it from any other, is just this: it destroys the old state apparatus as an instrument of denomination of the exploiting classes and in place of it creates a new organ of suppression of the exploiting minority by the majority, an organ of the organization and administration of the victorious people.

The formation of soviets in the course of the Revolution of 1905–1907 was the great historic achievement of the working class of Russia. This is shown by the fact that in 1917 the workers, soldiers, and peasants in the very beginning of the February Revolution formed soviets that served as the prototype of Soviet power, the state-form of the dictatorship of the proletariat that was established after the October Revolution in our country.

Few major participants in historic events have ever written about them with the professional qualifications of PAUL MILIUKOV (1859–1943). His prolific scholarly writing on Russian history began with a study of the financial policies of Peter the Great and include the popular, wide-ranging *Outlines of the History of Russian Culture*. While writing history, he was attempting also to make it, as a leader, perhaps *the* leader, of Russian liberalism. He was active in the formation of the Constitutional Democratic party (called "Kadet" after its Russian initials), which he represented in the Duma. The pinnacle of his political career came in early 1917 when he played the central role in forming the first Provisional Government, which he served briefly and unsuccessfully as minister of foreign affairs. To what extent does Miliukov's interpretation of the Duma period reveal the weakness of Russian liberalism and justify its critics of the Left and of the Right?*

Paul Miliukov

Liberal Disappointment in the Duma

The First Imperial Duma has been called "the Duma of popular indignation," but when it met on April 27, 1906, it was not so much "indignation" that filled the souls of the deputies. On that particular day their feelings were as radiant as the heavens are pure. It was as if they had forgotten all the unfavorable circumstances that had attended the convocation of the Duma: the imperfect electoral law, the publication of regulations limiting its powers, the malevolence of high officials of the government, and the distrust of the tsar. The deputies had only one thought, that they were participating in the convocation of the first Russian national parliament,

which was to make the laws that would change the old order and satisfy popular aspirations. In other words, they were to open the new era in Russian history that had been dreamed of for so long, to which so much effort had been devoted, so much blood shed. To make that dream a reality, everything else would be secondary, insignificant and easy to correct.

The opening session of the Duma took place in the Winter Palace. In the lavish surroundings of the imperial palace the deputies, dressed in frock coat or peasant dress, in national costume or the black soutane of the clergy, were framed by the courtiers in bemedaled uniforms. Under

*From a passage by Miliukov in Paul Milioukov, Ch. Seignobos, and L. Eisenmann, *Histoire de Russie (History of Russia)*, (Paris: Libraire Ernest Leroux, 1932), tome III, pp. 1131–1143, 1147–1151, 1155–1158. By permission of Presses Universitaires de France. Translated by Jacqueline F. McNeal.

the searching stares of the latter, the new-comers were able to sense the presence of an old, unfriendly world. But it was finished. Henceforth everything was going to change. Nor did the tsar refute this hope in his speech. "This memorable day," he concluded, "marks the beginning of the moral regeneration of Russia and the rebirth of her energies. I myself will insure the unshakable existence of the institutions that I have granted." . . .

The composition of the Duma was quite complex. At first there was some confusion, but little by little the lines were drawn more precisely and the deputies fell into nine distinct groups: 178 Kadets, 94 Trudoviks, 32 Poles, 26 Social Democrats [and others, of whom 100 did not belong to any group] . . .[1]

In effect the Trudoviks and Social Democrats thought of the Duma as an organ of revolutionary authority, very much like the Soviet of Workers' Deputies of 1905 or the more successful soviets of the second revolution [1917]. If this had been the conception of the Duma as a whole, its life would have been extremely short. Fortunately the Kadets, whose numbers and political experience made them the most important group, followed a less dangerous but more useful strategy, which it had previously determined at its congress. This party understood the absolute necessity of observing strict legality, even though it considered the new system of government far from perfect. They planned to set to work in the Duma and to prolong it for as long as possible in order to gradually ex-

tend the rights of the parliament. They therefore knew that they must avoid conflicts with the government when they had no legal basis, while utilizing the rights that had been conceded to the Duma. For example, they decided to raise the questions that were most important to the people, such as the agrarian question, and to seek a solution through strictly constitutional struggle, undeterred by eventual government opposition. In contrast to the Left, the Kadets did not count on immediate mass action to support the Duma because they realized that such action could not succeed unless it had been organized in advance and that the forces of revolution were losing their ability to carry out this organization. . . .

Dissent on the Left played into the hands of the government, which did not intend to treat the Duma seriously. From the start Premier Goremykin's policy was to ignore it. [I. L. Goremykin had replaced Witte on April 23, 1906.] Ministers did not show up at the Taurid Palace [the meeting place of the Duma], nor did they submit any legislative program. Only on May 15 did they submit their eternally famous first bill concerning the establishment of a laundry plant at the University of Dorpat. It seemed that the government's policy was to condemn the Duma to inaction—and Goremykin believed that the deputies' attitude would help him greatly, so that he could announce finally that the Duma is "unfit for work," the charge the deputies had leveled at him. But the Kadets were determined to act. Since they could not transform the Duma into a constituent assembly, they decided to undertake the enactment of reforms, without which the October Manifesto would remain illusory. They were prepared to submit a legislative program on their own initiative, although the fundamental law specified that bills could be debated only after a wait of one

[1] The Socialist Revolutionary party, which probably would have claimed the largest number of peasant votes, boycotted the elections to the First Duma, as did the Bolshevik Social Democrats. The "Trudovik" group in the Duma was not a party but a gathering of deputies from mainly rural constituencies who shared the goal of radical land reform. The Polish "circle" (Kolo) was also a collection of like-minded deputies who joined forces after the election.—Ed.

month, which was an eternity in the circumstances. Take, for example, the impatience of the journalist who in the first days of the Duma's existence declared at a meeting, "Three days have slipped by and the Duma has done nothing yet!" The majority of the Duma, with the Kadets, decided to begin work without delay. Well aware of their obligation to the masses, the deputies were ready to work day and night.

To follow correct constitutional procedure, the Duma began by drafting a reply to the tsar's speech at the Winter Palace, which it considered a speech from the throne. The Kadet's draft, with a few minor amendments by the Trudoviks, was approved unanimously. Six deputies of the moderate Right, including Count Heyden [an aristocratic advocate of reform for many years], abstained from these sessions so as not to weaken the effect of the unanimous vote. In this memorable resolution the Duma, confident in the promise that the tsar's concessions would remain "unshakable," presented a plan to assure the progressive, normal development of Russia: universal suffrage; abrogation of the laws that granted emergency powers, which concealed administrative arbitrariness; extension of the Duma's right to initiate budgetary action and legislation in agreement with the tsar, who legally possessed the initiative on these matters; precise laws on individual liberty, freedom of conscience, speech, press, association and assembly, the right to strike, the equality of all citizens before the law and the removal of all special rights of class, nationality, religion, and sex; abolition of capital punishment; settlement of the agrarian problem on the principle of enforced confiscation of [nonpeasant] land; recognition of the rightful claims of the diverse nationalities; finally, formation of a cabinet responsible to the Duma, to end at last the power of the bureaucrats who separated the tsar

from his people, and to assure the harmonious collaboration of the legislative and executive functions. The Duma named a delegation to present the tsar with this address, which could not possibly be considered revolutionary because it avoided all the subversive proposals of the extreme Left.

The constitutional parties hoped that the interview with the tsar would strengthen their position vis-à-vis the cabinet. But after three days of feverish waiting the Duma learned from Goremykin that the tsar had refused to receive its delegation. With some difficulty, the Kadets succeeded in persuading the workers not to make this a pretext for revolt. On May 13, in the presence of all the members of the cabinet, who on this occasion made their first appearance in the Duma, Goremykin read to the deputies the government's reply to their address. . . .

This reply, delivered in the tone of a lecture, was a declaration of war. It deeply pained the more moderate deputies, like Count Heyden, who declared that the refusal of the premier destroyed all hopes of peaceful collaboration. . . .

It was not without some hesitation that the government decided on dissolution of the Duma. Most of the deputies were convinced that the Duma would not be touched. The leftists in particular claimed that simply by existing it had prevented the outbreak of revolution, and the premier was not far from believing, with the Trudoviks, that the people would refuse to accept quietly the news of its dissolution. For this reason the ministerial entourage and especially the tsar's court were interested in the possibility of an agreement with the moderate members of educated society. When D. N. Shipov [a liberal long active in the zemstvo of Tver province] was approached, he refused to negotiate, stating with his customary frankness that he did not represent the majority. In an audience that the tsar granted him, he advised negotiations with the Kadets, the leading party in the Duma, and suggested a combination of P. N. Miliukov and S. A. Muromtsev [a Kadet, chairman of the Duma]. In keeping with his practice when faced with ideas contrary to his own, the tsar questioned Shipov closely and seemed to share his views, pretending to appreciate the advantages of dealing with the persons he proposed. At the tsar's order some meetings did take place between Miliukov and Stolypin. The result clearly showed that the government did not dream of a purely Kadet cabinet, or of concessions that would satisfy the majority in the Duma. The talks, which were undertaken on a purely personal basis, only because of the mood of the Duma, were broken off as soon as it was apparent that no agreement was possible between the government, which contested even the existence of a constitution, and the constitutional party of the Duma.

The cabinet then decided on dissolution. Since Goremykin could not reconcile himself to this dangerous step, execution of the order was finally entrusted to Stolypin, who became premier. He took military precautions, not only in the capital but throughout the empire. It appears that the date for dissolution was chosen only at the last moment. During the Duma session of Friday, July 2, Stolypin asked the chairman to schedule his reply to an interpellation concerning the Belostok pogrom for Monday, July 10. But on Sunday, July 9 [1906], the deputies who came to the Taurid Palace in the afternoon found the doors closed and guarded by sentries, while larger military forces with artillery occupied the neighboring streets to prevent any uprising. . . .

Stolypin was greatly concerned with preparations for the elections to the Second Duma. If he kept the old electoral law, he was determined to use all means to render it harmless. In this he had an eager helper in Krizhanovsky, deputy minister of internal affairs, who was experienced in putting pressure on the voter's spirit without touching the letter of the law; the Senate [a supreme court] also helped with "interpretations" that changed the law. . . .

What was the result of these maneuvers? The extreme Right elected 63 deputies; the moderate Right, or Octobrist party, 34; Kadets 123; Poles 39; Trudoviks, 97; the socialist parties 83. Twenty-two deputies were unaffiliated. Despite its efforts, the government had been unable to assure the election of a docile majority. . . .

Although the Second Duma was somewhat more radical than the First, the mood of all the opposition parties had changed markedly since the dissolution of July 1906. The radiant hopes that had been aroused by the opening of the First Duma had vanished. It was understood that the representatives of the nation were not inviolable and that the government could easily destroy this frail instrument without any popular reaction. The Second Duma was therefore less concerned with defending its power than with maintaining its very existence. It realized that it would last only, more or less, as long as it could avoid mortal conflicts. "Save the Duma" was the watchword that the socialist parties themselves adopted tacitly, while publicly reproaching the Kadets for suggesting it. For its part, the government did not want an immediate collision with the Duma. On the contrary, by submitting some bills and the budget to the secretariat of the Duma it showed its desire to collaborate.

The first obstacle to be surmounted was the government's proclamation, read by Stolypin on March 6 [1907]. So as not to deliver a vote of disapproval that would furnish the pretext for its immediate dissolution, the Duma adopted the strategy of silence, which was interrupted only by the

Social Democrats. Furthermore, the proclamation that commented on the proposed legislative program was moderate in tone. It even acknowledged that the Duma could amend government bills. Only in his speech in answer to the Social Democrats, whom he plainly separated from the other parties of the opposition, was Stolypin more uncompromising. He declared that "the will of the sovereign has not authorized the Duma to express its defiance of the government," and he ended with the exclamation, "You will not frighten us!" . . .

On June 3 [1907] the Duma was dissolved, new elections were fixed for September 1, and convocation of the Third Duma for November 1. At the same time a new electoral law was published, although it could not really be considered a law since it was a direct violation of the fundamental laws, which required that the Duma consent to modification of the electoral law. The parties of the Right were triumphant, scarcely concealing that from the constitutional point of view this was a veritable *coup d'état*. For them it was more than proof that there was no Russian constitution. "The tsar giveth, the tsar taketh away," summed up their feelings. The accusations that the manifesto of June 3 made against the Duma were without foundation. In reality its great crime was that it would not disavow the revolutionary terror and that at the same time it refused its moral support to the government. The publication of a new electoral law left no doubt about the strong, though unacknowledged, motives for dissolution. The law could not have been drafted in one night. It was the result of an agreement between the nobility and the government. Not by simple coincidence was the Duma dissolved just at the moment when Krizhanovsky's masterpiece of the electoral art [rigged electoral laws] left the printing presses. The country was

not fooled. It understood that the Second Duma had been purely and simply sacrificed to the interests of the nobility. . . .

The *"chambre introuvable"* [that the new, rigged electoral law produced] was profoundly different from the First Duma, being composed in large measure of supporters of the government. The government majority combined three rightist groups, the nationalists and the Octobrists, having over 300 deputies out of a total of 442. The opposition, led by the Kadets, was reduced to a little more than 100 members . . . The majority adopted the name "government bloc." The Octobrists took the lead, pursuing a policy of "pacification and reforms." As prisoners of the parties to their Right, wishing to curry favor with the government that had assured their victory, the Octobrists proved themselves to be the worst "constitutionalists." The majority declared the members of the opposition to be enemies of the country, accused them of fomenting the destruction of the state, of being subject to the pernicious influence of the Jews. The government bloc also cast suspicion on the national ethnic groups (Polish and Moslem) as well as on representatives from other alien ethnic groups. Not only the speakers from the Right, but also those from the centrist Octobrists unsparingly attacked the whole opposition and the Kadets in particular. . . . Opposition deputies were excluded from the war and navy committees on the pretext that they were not patriotic. Finally the atmosphere became so vile, the abusive campaign against some of these deputies so vitriolic, the insults so shameless, that the position of the opposition speakers became quite painful. Interrupted by outrageous remarks and organized noise from the extreme Right benches, they had great difficulty in presenting their ideas. In the third session [1911], however, relations between the opposition and the Octobrists improved rather considerably. The latter began to show more tolerance toward those of their opponents who were acknowledged specialists and eminent parliamentarians. When the Octobrists wanted to work out their program on technical points — budgetary reform, development of the army, the introduction of certain liberal reforms of incontestable value, such as local justice and public education, and extension of zemstvo institutions — they recognized that they had to depend on help from the opposition parties.

For over a generation BERNARD PARES (1867–1949) was the best-known Russian specialist in the English-speaking world. From the opening of the twentieth century until the Revolution of 1917 he spent a good part of his life in Russia, which he loved and knew to a degree attained by few if any Westerners in the present generation. He was particularly intimate with Duma liberals, whom he admired and criticized. After the revolution he founded the School of Slavonic and East European Studies of the University of London, the first institution of this sort in the English-speaking world. His general *History of Russia* continues to be one of the more widely read books on the subject. Pares' other works include *Russia and Reform,* which was influential in the English-speaking world for years, and *My Russian Memoirs,* which give the reader both an account of his experiences in Russia and a good idea of his Victorian-liberal perspective on life.*

Bernard Pares

Liberal Optimism Concerning the Duma

There is no need here to dwell on the short life of the First Duma. It was indeed the cream of the Russian intelligentsia and the peasants in particular had obeyed the imperial summons to choose men who had the confidence of the population and were generally too shrewd to be led away by party cries. But the revolutionary basis on which the success of the reformers had so much depended, had fallen away from beneath them; the country was sick of revolution. So few were the competent public men in Russia that the elections to the Duma depleted the zemstva of most of their best men. The Cadets never had a

basis of organization in the country; there was no real possibility of frequent public meetings, and they had only insignificant party funds. Hardly any of them had any experience of administration; they were mostly professional men who hoped to carry the fortress of autocracy by expressions of principle.

The first and best act of the Duma was to put the needs of the country clearly before the sovereign. Adopting English precedents—as it did, not only now, but throughout its existence—the Duma replied to "the King's Speech" made to it by the Emperor when receiving it at the

*Reprinted with omissions and transliterations of Russian names by permission of the publisher from *The Fall of the Russian Monarchy,* by Bernard Pares, pp. 94–97, 100–106, 117–119. First published in the United States by Alfred A. Knopf, Inc., 1939. Vintage edition, 1961. Also reprinted with the permission of the Executors of the Bernard Pares Estate. The dates have been changed from the "new" style to the "old."

Winter Palace and containing little more than general expressions of good will, by an "Address to the Throne"—such was the title actually chosen. It was drafted so ably as to carry the support of all the different groups in the House, it was steered through the debate with exceptional ability by the young Liberal, Vladimir Nabokov and was adopted almost unanimously. While embracing all the main demands of the public, it was capable of circulation throughout Russia in microscopic form on a post card. Much fuss was made by the Government as to whether the Duma had a right to address the sovereign, but it was ultimately received by the Minister of the Court. Goremykin then led his heterogeneous colleagues down to the Duma and read a lecture, after the manner of an old schoolmaster, in which he dismissed the most important demand of all, relating to land for the peasants, as "inadmissible." Nabokov at once proposed a vote of censure, and this led to a debate in which one abuse of the Government after another was laid bare. The Ministers present, with the exception of Stolypin, proved quite incapable of defending themselves, being as new to this environment as anyone else.

So far everything had proceeded on the English model, and after the vote of censure presumably the Government ought to resign. It did not do so, and Government and Duma sat looking at each other, each wondering what step it dared to take, and what support it would receive from the country. Ultimately, in order to win such support, the Duma raised the land question in two Bills, respectively from the Cadet and Labor [Trudovik] Parties, both of which were based on the principle of compulsory expropriation of land: the first with compensation and the second without. The Government next invited the peasants to look to it for support rather than to the Duma. The Duma now decided to make its own appeal to the country, but this was precisely one of those things which the fundamental laws forbade it to do.

With the Government there was a crisis of indecision. [The conservative] Trepov, who had the ear of the Emperor, actually advised him to treat with the Liberals and call them to office, and it is almost clear from a half finished utterance of his that he hoped they would find the task of governing too difficult for them, and would pave the way for a military dictatorship. Stolypin, on the other hand, who defined his position as "a constitutionalist (under the Manifesto of October), but not a parliamentarist," urged that a Cadet Ministry would in a few months have destroyed all the prestige of the Government, and that the loss would be irreparable. Stolypin was for dissolving this Duma under the existing law and calling another under the same conditions. It is significant that the strongest plea against dissolution was made by the Foreign Minister, Izvolsky, recently appointed to direct Russian foreign policy towards friendship with France and England. The Emperor had long been yearning to dissolve the Duma, in which of course he had the full support of Goremykin. He was not prepared for a "leap into the unknown" and he felt that in face of the challenge to his authority, resistance at all costs was better than surrender. He still hesitated and consulted various advisers. Kokovtsev strongly counselled against any adoption of English parliamentarism. Stolypin had negotiated with some of the leading "public men" for what was to be called later a "Ministry of Confidence," a blend of the more reasonable holders of office with men who represented the more moderate shades of public opinion. Trepov and Izvolsky were frankly for a cabinet composed exclusively of the latter with Muromtsev, the President of the Duma, at its head. Muromtsev was indeed approached — as he understood, on behalf of the sovereign. He referred the matter to Miliukov as leader of the dominant party in the Duma. Shipov, who was also approached, had but few supporters in the Duma and gave the same answer. Miliukov was out to carry the whole position by moral pressure and demanded a Cadet Ministry, with himself at its head. Here he made one of the crucial mistakes of his career. Conversation had passed between Trepov and Miliukov, and Miliukov has himself owned to having "set very hard conditions." It was in the middle of this that the Duma decided to appeal to the public against the Government, which Miliukov had done his best to prevent; and it was this appeal which finally decided the Emperor. On July 7th the Cabinet was summoned for 8 p.m. Goremykin and Stolypin had been sent for, separately, to Tsarskoe Selo. Goremykin was received first and advised the appointment of Stolypin as Prime Minister and the dissolution of the Duma; and he returned to the Cabinet in the mood—as he put it, of "a schoolboy on holiday"—to announce this decision, which was published directly afterwards.

The Duma continued to rely on its moral strength and on the country. The Cadets and the Labor Party made a hurried dash for Viborg over the Finnish border—an act of half bravery very prejudicial to the liberties of Finland—and there adopted an appeal to the country to demand that the dissolution be withdrawn—clearly an unconstitutional act, as the sovereign unquestionably had the right to dissolve. In the meantime, until the Duma was restored, they called on the country to refuse recruits to the army and taxes to the Treasury, and to recognize no foreign loans contracted in its absence. There was no organization to carry out this programme and the initiative was left to any given village. It was a piece of political bluff. The country was in a state of inertia and took no action. . . .

When, however, the Second Duma met on February 20th, 1907, the effects of the Viborg exclusions were painfully manifest. Russia was anyhow weak enough in trained politicians, and its parliamentary experience was confined to the First Duma, which was now excluded almost wholesale. The Cadets, who had led in the First Duma, were now represented in the main by secondary men, with the notable exceptions of Rodichev, who had been in England when the Viborg appeal was signed, and two new men, Andrew Shingarev and Basil Maklakov, who were to play distinguished parts later. Shingarev was a model provincial medical officer trained in the work of the county councils, upright, intelligent and clear-headed, who was to grow beyond recognition in the atmosphere of the Duma. Maklakov, one of the most brilliant members of the Russian bar, had a natural gift of oratory which, under the discipline which he gave to it, developed into a real political power. This time the revolutionary parties entered the Duma under their own flags, as Social Democrats or Social Revolutionaries. There was also a small group of reactionaries, largely pushed through by police pressure, including a most remarkable die-hard, Vladimir Purishkevich, and a brilliant young Conservative, Basil Shulgin.

The reactionaries, now triumphant and even exultant, were out to destroy the Duma altogether. Their tactics were crude and simple; they determined to compromise it before Russian and foreign opinion by raising as often as possible in debate the question of terrorism. The Duma was there to perform such duties as examining the credits for building railways or making bridges, and all theoretical subjects lay outside its competence, except by inference. However, the challenge was one which many revolutionaries in the Duma could not refrain from taking up, and on May 30th the subject was debated in full. The Duma contained no less than nine different parties, and each put forward its own theoretical view. None was accepted, and the House remained without an answer to this burning question.

Meanwhile the police had been busy in the same cause and announced, one after the other, the discovery of two plots implicating the two main revolutionary parties, the S.R.s and the S.D.s. [Socialist Revolutionaries and Social Democrats]. The charges were widely debated at the time, but it was only after the revolution of 1917 that the full publication of police details on the subject has proved conclusively the provocative character of both plots; in fact the manoeuvre was later brought in its nakedness before the Cabinet and severely condemned. . . .

Stolypin had done what he could to find a working basis with the Second Duma; as he said ironically at the time, it was taking him more trouble to prevent the dissolution of the Second Duma than to obtain the dissolution of the First. . . . The Emperor was waiting with the greatest impatience for a chance of dissolving it; he was infuriated by a speech full of insults to the Russian army. Stolypin had to demand a special sitting to debate the Shornikova plot [the framed evidence used to inculpate the Social Democrats] and to obtain the surrender of the S.D. members [of the Duma]. The Duma refused to deprive them of their immunity from arrest as Members without further investigation of the charge, and while a commission for the purpose was hastily examining the evidence, the Second Duma was dissolved. The President, F. A. Golovin, himself only learned the news from a journalist.

Troops had been brought into St. Petersburg; and the second dissolution was taken lying down both by the Duma and by the country, except for sporadic disorders. An imperial manifesto accused the Duma of having plotted against the sovereign, and this was followed up almost immediately by the publication of a new electoral law, which abolished all semblance of universal suffrage and threw the elections for the most part into the hands of a dying class, the country gentry. The one saving clause, not noticed by either side at the time, was that no change was made in the competence of the Duma, which still remained a legislative body, though the Emperor from this time onwards more than once contemplated reducing its functions to consultation only. . . .

The change in the electoral law was essentially a *coup d'état*. The new law preposterous. Of the towns, where voting had been direct, nearly all lost their members, and were merged in the country constituencies; where the town representation was retained, all the electors were divided into two categories, monstrously unequal, each of which elected to the same number of seats; on the one side were the owners of large property, on the other all the rest, including of course the professional class. A member for the first of these categories in St. Petersburg, when I asked him how he could explain a certain step of his to his constituents, replied: "My constituents could all be gathered together in one room." In the country the centre of gravity was completely shifted to the country gentry; this was done by giving them, though they were only a sprinkling, a majority of the "electors." Thus even the peasant members of the Third and Fourth Dumas were really elected by the gentry. . . .

This wholesale falsification of the principle of election did not look as if it could lead to anything good; yet those who knew Russia at the time could be sure that practically any national assembly would be in opposition to the Government, even if it had consisted exclusively of ex-Ministers. Stolypin, on his side, had made every effort to broaden the basis of his Cabinet by negotiating with such public men as [the Right-wing liberals] Guchkov, Nicholas Lvov and Paul Vinogradov; but though in some cases he induced them to visit the sovereign, such men were bound in conscience to refuse, because it was quite impossible for them to get even a minimum of guarantee that the principles which they represented would be respected, so that they could only have been regarded as individual captives of the reaction. . . .

Yet this phase did not last long. The disillusionment acted as a cold douche. There were some very remarkable Liberal political thinkers at this time, and they set themselves to examine with absolute honesty the causes of their failure. "The power," wrote Peter Struve, "dropped from our unprepared hands." The remedy they found in a deepening of personal discipline, a deeper understanding of the issues involved and the forces opposed to them. Meanwhile the more intelligent members of the public set about such practical work as could at least extend their activity in the management of their own affairs. The politicians explored the situation to see what was left that could still be saved out of the wreck. There was a very great deal. There was still some kind of a national assembly, which could not fail in some respect to reflect the opinions and interests of the country. If the franchise of the Duma had been radically altered, its competence remained untouched, and it was still a legislative assembly. The first two Dumas in their heat and haste had let themselves be dissolved without living long enough to use their most powerful weapon,

the yearly examination of the budget, which involved prolonged and public discussion of all important questions. The parliamentary reports were ordinarily still exempt from the censorship; indeed, there were numbers of peasants who learned to read from the Duma debates. No party made more use of the Duma as a forum than the Social Democrats.

All these conditions were acutely appreciated by the new man of the moment, Alexander Guchkov. The Cadets had had their period and they had failed hopelessly. Their leader, Paul Miliukov, was too doctrinaire to lead an attack in detail. Guchkov, grandson of a serf, son of a merchant and magistrate of Moscow, was a restless spirit always coming into prominence on this or that issue of the moment, now going through Macedonia or Armenia in times of disorders, now riding along the Great Wall of China at the time of the Boxers' rising, now fighting for the Boers against England in South Africa, now remaining in Mukden to transfer the care of the wounded to the advancing Japanese, now returning to say a bold word for enlightened and patriotic Conservatism in the whirl of 1905, now summoned and entertained by the Emperor and Empress and fearlessly advising the Tsar to establish a link between himself and his people by summoning some kind of national assembly, though his ideas then hardly went beyond the old Zemsky Sobor of the 16th and 17th centuries.

Guchkov's chief quality was a daring gallantry; he was at ease with himself and enjoyed stepping forward under fire with a perfect calm whenever there was anything which he wished to challenge; his defect was his restlessness; without actually asking for it, he was instinctively always in the limelight, always trying to do too much. He had the easy organizing ability of a first-rate English politician; he was quietly proud of his democratic origin, and all his actions were inspired by an ardent love for Russia and the Russian people, in whose native conservatism, common sense and loyalty he fully shared. He was an enemy of class privileges, and at this time he claimed for his country some such measure of consultation as was secured for Germany by the Reichstag. Guchkov led the Octobrists or party of patriotic reform, and for them no less than for the Cadets the political model was England; but while the Cadets preached English political principles, the Octobrists were much more akin to the ordinary instincts of English public life. . . .

May an Englishman, bred in the tradition of Gladstone, to whom the Duma was almost a home with many friends of all parties, recall that vanished past? At the bottom was a feeling of reassurance, and founded on it one saw a growing courage and initiative and a growing mutual understanding and goodwill. The Duma had the freshness of a school, with something of surprise at the simplicity with which differences that had seemed formidable could be removed. One could feel the pleasure with which the Members were finding their way into common work for the good of the whole country. In the First Duma peasants had picked out as their chief impression the realization that Russia was a great family, that there were so many others with thoughts and hopes like their own. "It went past like a dream" one of them said to me. The Second Duma was fast growing more and more into a family when it was prematurely dissolved. The Third Duma, though its horizon was much more limited, did come to stay, and its membership was better qualified to take practical advantage of the education which it offered. Some seventy persons at least, forming the nucleus of the more important commissions, were learning in detail to understand

the problems and difficulties of administration and therefore to understand both each other and the Government. One could see political competence growing day by day. And to a constant observer it was becoming more and more an open secret that the distinctions of party meant little, and that in the social warmth of their public work for Russia all these men were becoming friends.

The most perceptible success of the Duma so far lay in the creation of an atmosphere of confidence. The Duma was establishing itself as an indispensable part of the organization of public life, and the Emperor himself took a certain pride in it as his own creation. Those surrounding him continued their attempts to prejudice it in his eyes, but having once rejected the occasion to abolish it in his *coup d'état* of 1907, he was increasingly less likely to do so now. In 1912 he said to me: "The Duma started too fast; now it is slower, but better," and in answer to a rather audacious question he added benevolently: "And more lasting." That was the general judgment of others, and the result was a growing vigour of initiative not only in practical affairs, but also in thought and expression. The censorship was subject to criticism in the Duma, and at no time did it work with more respect for public opinion. In the provinces, it is true, there continued to be monstrous cases of arbitrary fines imposed by the local governors. Though there was no preliminary censorship, the iniquitous provision of the so-called press reform of Alexander II still obtained, by which newspapers could be crushed with such fines by the administrative officials. In the capital, however, it was very different; and serious monthlies, such as even *Byloe (The Past)* of the revolutionary Burtsev, could be published freely. Criticism took heart; and the Russian mind, with its quick intelligence and biting humour, is peculiarly effective in criticism. Also, great works of scholarship began to be published, such as the inimitable history of Russia by Kliuchevsky, which though full of intelligent patriotism and religion, had so far only circulated in notes of students. Typically enough, the first volume came out in the year of the First Duma. The practical removal of a ban on many great works of scientific and statistical study meant an enormous increase of the intellectual wealth of the country.

Since Stalin's death Soviet historical studies have given
increasing attention to the conservative side of the political
spectrum in Russia prior to World War I. Although there
has been no trend toward un-Leninist interpretations, the
very existence of detailed scholarship in this area
represents an improvement since Stalin's time. Perhaps the
outstanding specialist among the younger historians who
have contributed to this development is ARON
IAKOVLEVICH AVREKH of Moscow State University,
author of the most ambitious study of the politics of the
Duma period to appear in the Soviet Union, entitled
Stolypin and the Third Duma. He has also published shorter
works on *Tsarism and the June Third Monarchy,* "The June
Third Monarchy and the Labor Question," and "V. I.
Lenin on the Revolutionary Situation." To what extent
does his interpretation resemble Miliukov's, despite the
obvious gulf between Communists and liberals?*

Aron Iakovlevich Avrekh

The Failure of Stolypin's Tyranny

By the summer of 1907 the revolution
finally had been suppressed and the period
that has gone down in the history of Russia
as "the Stolypin reaction" began. As the
writer V. G. Korolenko so vividly put it,
the death sentence became "part of the
way of life." Many who escaped the death
sentence perished at forced labor or in pris-
on. The country was governed not according to the normal order, but on an emergency basis, under the "Decree on Means
for Protecting State Security and Social
Tranquility" of August 14, 1881. The
main blow was struck against the working
class and its party. Bolshevik organizations
were subjected to merciless destruction. Almost all eminent participants in revolutionary social democracy had emigrated or
were in jail. The party underwent a serious crisis and was obliged to carry on the
fight under conditions of disrupted com
munications, continual gaps in its ranks,
and the absence of financial support.
Nonetheless, the Bolsheviks were able to
come out of this crisis with minimum
losses, retaining their organization and discipline to the maximum extent possible.
The petty-bourgeois parties were in a condition of complete disintegration and disorganization, splitting into separate groups
and trends.

Under the blows of police persecution
and in the circumstances of an industrial
depression, the strike movement declined

*From A. L. Sidorov (ed.), *Istoriia SSSR,* tom II, *1861–1917, Period kapitalizma (History of the
USSR,* vol. II, *The Period of Capitalism)* (Moscow: Mysl', second edition, 1965), pp. 453–454, 455–461,
468–470, 472–473. Translated by Robert H. McNeal.

sharply. In 1910 the number of strikers fell to 46,000, and most of the strikes were predominantly defensive, as the capitalists took the offensive everywhere and tried to regain what the workers had won in 1905. Weakened by punitive expeditions and the arrest of active participants in the attacks on landlords and the government, the peasantry, too, had a hard time. From 1906 to 1912 over 600 trade unions were closed and about the same number were denied legal registration. About a thousand newspapers and magazines were closed.

Decadent literature circulated widely, its favorite themes being suicide, betrayal, debauchery. Many writers, such as Artsybashev, Igor, Severianin, Verbitskaia, mocked the ideals of social progress, sowed the seeds of disbelief and despair. These poisoned ideas caused great harm, especially among the youth.

On June 3, 1907, the tsar's manifesto on the dissolution of the Second Duma and the new electoral law was published. This act infringed the October Manifesto, the decree of December 11, 1905, and the "Fundamental Law" of 1906. . . .

The *coup d'état* of June 3 demonstrated the full measure of the victory of the counterrevolution, the colonialist-nationalist policy of tsarism and the Russian bourgeoisie, their hatred and fear of the revolutionary movement. The government mobilized all its resources to rig the election campaign in its favor. Deception, falsification of electoral lists, arrests and "withdrawals" of undesirable candidates, and so on were widely practiced. The capitalists forbade the workers to assemble in the factories to elect their lawful electors to serve in the provincial electoral assemblies. The right to hold election campaign meetings and to electioneer was granted only to landlord and bourgeois organizations and parties. The election yielded the results that were envisaged by the new electoral law. The party

composition of the Third Duma soon after it opened on November 1, 1907, was: extreme Right wing, 50; Russian nationalists and moderate rightists, 97; Octobrists and close associates, 154; Progressivists, 28; Kadets, 54; Moslems, 9; Poles, White Russians, and Lithuanians, 18; Trudoviks, 13; Social Democrats, 20. . . .

The numerical composition of the Duma was such that the outcome of voting depended on the Octobrists. If they voted with the rightists, there was a rightist-Octobrist majority; if they voted with the progressivists and Kadets, then there was a different majority. The first majority numbered about 300, the second 250. This was not accidental. "The electoral law of the Third Duma," wrote V. I. Lenin, "was so arranged that these two majorities were obtained."

For what purpose did tsarism require two majorities in the Duma? This was called for by the same causes that inspired [Stolypin's agrarian reform] decree of November 9: the need for allies and the transition to bourgeois monarchy. If the Stolypin decree constituted a first step of tsarism toward bourgeois monarchy, in the realm of economics, then the June 3 Duma was a second step, in the field of the political superstructure. Concretely it signified the attempt of tsarism to rule the country with the aid of representative institutions—the Duma.

One of the results of the revolution for tsarism was that a return to the former "pure" autocracy, without the Duma, was impossible. Any parliament, however restricted its rights might be — and the Duma was just such a parliament — could only be a bourgeois institution by its nature and by the goals in a society dominated by capitalist relations. "The autocracy," wrote V. I. Lenin, "tried to take on the completion of the objectively necessary tasks of the bourgeois revolution — the establishment of popular representation, actually of managing the affairs of bourgeois society." In other words, the Third Duma represented a political alliance of tsarism and the bourgeoisie. Previously such an alliance had existed on a limited scale and in the main had not taken shape politically. Now the situation had changed. "The Third Duma," wrote V. I. Lenin "is the politically formed, all-national union of political organizations of landlords and the wealthy bourgeoisie." The basis of the alliance of the bourgeoisie and tsarism was the counterrevolutionary character common to both partners.

The bourgeoisie was no less counterrevolutionary than tsarism. In the words of V. I. Lenin, "It feared revolution more than reaction." This caused it to be ready to play the role in the alliance of assistant and adviser of "historically constituted authority," satisfied, for its part, by the promises of the minimal bourgeois reforms. At the same time the bourgeoisie manifested an organic attraction to tsarism because of its vital economic interests. For the most part it was still "the plunderer of the epoch of primitive accumulation," striving in its commercial and industrial activities first to "grab a good slice of the tax-revenue pie, in the form of guaranties, subsidies, concessions, protective tariffs, etc." Government orders and contracts were by far the most seductive free market for the Russian bourgeoisie, and they proposed to gain foreign markets not by the cheapness or attractiveness of their goods but by the aid of colonial expansion — that long-established policy of tsarism.

In turn, tsarism needed the bourgeoisie as a force for the industrial and financial development of the country and, consequently, for national military strength. This explains why tsarism so willingly granted subsidies to large enterprises, introduced high protective tariffs, conducted a policy of favoritism, especially to heavy industry, metallurgy, coal mining and oil, which brought the bourgeoisie colossal superprofits. The bourgeoisie was necessary to tsarism as a guarantor of foreign loans. The Duma, or more precisely its bourgeois part, approving the tsarist budget and demonstrating the unity of the "social forces" with the "historically constituted authority," served as such a guarantee. In addition the Duma had to serve as a "constitutional" façade of tsarism, summoned up to provide a mask for absolutism, both for the populace of Russia and the outside world.

But the alliance of tsarism and the bourgeoisie concealed profound internal contradictions. Tsarism tried to use the Duma in order to preserve its political omnipotence. The bourgeoisie, despite its fear of revolution, continually aimed at sharing power with tsarism, and this meant conflicts between the two concerning the means and the forms of bourgeois reform.

Because tsarism exercised hegemony in the conditions of the June 3 monarchy, it arranged things so as to exclude the real possibility that the Duma could conduct an independent policy. First, tsarism succeeded in reducing to naught the budgetary and legislative rights of the Duma by making the ministers wholly independent of the Duma, responsible only to the tsar, and by making the second chamber, the Council of State, the legislative equal of the Duma. No bill passed by the Duma could become law if rejected by the Council of State. Finally, any bill passed by both chambers could still fail to become law if the tsar withheld approval. "The June 3 system," emphasized V. I. Lenin, "especially counted on the utilization in a very wide area of the antagonisms between the liberal bourgeoisie and the reactionary landlords, which existed along with the common, much deeper antagonism of both toward all democracy and the working class in particular."

This calculation was embodied in the Duma with its two majorities. The rightist-Octobrist majority was to play the main role—to conduct a conservative policy, to strengthen the foundations of autocracy. But the government needed the other, Kadet-Octobrist majority, which to a certain extent would oppose the Right, landlord portion of the Duma, and would secure passage of the minimal bourgeois reforms without which the Duma would lose its point as an instrument that was needed to secure the transition of tsarism to a bourgeois monarchy. "The government," wrote V. I. Lenin, "needs the liberal-Octobrist majority in order to try to lead Russia forward under the preservation of the omnipotence of the Purishkeviches" [the ultra-Right].

The characteristic of the Octobrist "Center," which played the role of an oscillating pendulum, forming mutually contradictory majorities, was rooted in the class nature of the Octobrists. By its composition and dominant attitude it was a party of the Right. Three-quarters of the "Union of October 17" consisted of the same social elements that comprised the rightist groups. At the same time, the party was the creation of the wealthy bourgeoisie, mainly drawn from Muscovite commerce and industry, and its program was bourgeois in content, demanding the implementation, in a sharply curtailed version, to be sure, of the "principles" of the October Manifesto. As evident in its name, the party made this manifesto its banner. The leader of the Octobrists was A. I. Guchkov, a typical representative of Muscovite capitalism.

It was not accidental that two elements rooted in different social classes were joined in one party. On the contrary, this was conditioned by their common political and economic interests, their striving to gain satisfaction of their demands not with the aid of parliamentarianism (the subordination of the government to the legislative institutions) but by means of a direct deal with tsarism. Moreover, the feudal landlords and the bourgeoisie were linked by thousands of economic and political ties. The Muscovite and other industrial bosses did not go much beyond their brother-landlords in their methods of exploitation. In their methods of struggle with the revolutionary movement, the solution of the national question, and many other questions, they differed little from the rightists and nationalists. In turn, the feudal landlords were closely linked with capitalists and capitalism, and as they gradually evolved on the "Prussian" path of development [the growth of large farms run on a capitalist basis], they became interested in the Octobrist reforms. The prevailing rightist, landlord part of the party dominated its bourgeois part. Guchkov and his policy actually depended on the rightists, and especially on Stolypin. Thus did the Octobrist Duma fraction play the role of the so-called Center, that is, the main, party. The Octobrists were the government party in the sense that they subordinated their policy to the will of the government and were the tool of Stolypin's policy. This meant that the first, rightist-Octobrist majority dominated the second, and within the first majority the Right wing was dominant.

In turn, the Octobrists were in command within the second majority. On the eve of the opening of the Third Duma, the fifth congress of the Kadet party adopted a resolution in favor of supporting liberal bills "whencesoever they may originate," "and bills that could command a majority in the Third Duma could originate from no source other than the Octobrists," wrote V. I. Lenin. To emphasize their difference in principle from the Social Democrats, the Kadets declared themselves the "responsible opposition," that is, an opposition that participates in "organic legislation."

The policy of the Kadet party was embodied in its leader, P. N. Miliukov, an eminent historian and an agile and resourceful politician who gained a deserved reputation as a political Jesuit. He took great pains to conceal from the masses the true meaning of Kadet policy, to preserve for the party the mask of "Constitutional Democracy," the party of "the People's Freedom." But these policies were in vain. The Kadets revealed in full measure their subservience to the Octobrists and tsarism.

In the summer of 1909 Miliukov, while visiting England as a member of a "parliamentary" visit of a group of members of the Duma and Council of State, declared at a dinner given by the lord mayor of London that "while there is in Russia a legislative chamber that controls the budget, the Russian opposition remains the opposition of His Majesty and not to His Majesty." This servile statement, which proclaimed a bloody despot to be a constitutional monarch, in hopes of thereby receiving some "reforms," also served to show that the Kadets no longer entertained illusions about their actual influence on the masses.

Thus the June 3 system was created by a government coup. Just such a system was the initial political prerequisite of Stolypin's Bonapartist course. V. I. Lenin defined the essence of Bonapartism as follows: "Bonapartism is the maneuvering of a monarchy that has lost its old, patriarchal or feudal, simple and solid base—monarchy that is obliged to balance, so as not to fall, to cajole in order to govern, to bribe in order to be liked, to fraternize with the dregs of

society, with plain thieves and swindlers, in order to be supported not merely by bayonets. . ."

In the spring of 1909 the dissatisfaction of the higher-ups [*verkhi*—which in this usage seems deliberately vague] and the tsarist camarilla with Stolypin reached such proportions that they decided to overthrow him. In this connection a so-called ministerial crisis was unleashed, expressed in a noisy campaign of accusations that Stolypin, supposedly with the Octobrists, had made up his mind to confer on the ministers and the Duma many of the prerogatives of the supreme authority. The pretext for unleashing this crisis was a minor bill on the budget of the naval general staff, which was introduced into the Duma by the minister of the navy. In May 1908 the bill was passed by the Duma but rejected by the Council of State. In the opinion of the Council, the Duma had the right to approve only sums that were requested and not the budget itself [the allocation of parts of the sum to various recipients], for the army and navy were subordinate only to the tsar, who was by fundamental law the supreme commander of the army. In answer to this, the Duma, which considered the bill to be urgent, adopted it on December 8, 1909 in the same form as before. Applying great pressure, Stolypin succeeded in putting the bill through the Council of State, but the premier's position became so shaky that all the newspapers began to write of his impending fall. At the same time the rightiest press subjected the Octobrists, headed by Guchkov, to furious attacks. They were called "Russian Young Turks," that is, persons striving to take power by a military coup. Stolypin succeeded in remaining in power only at the price of complete capitulation to the camarilla and the Right. . . .

In the years of Stolypin's regime the policy of persecution of the non-Russian peoples reached its extreme limits. The Manifesto of June 3 had already demanded that the Duma be "Russian in spirit." The object of this policy was to poison the masses with nationalist fumes, to combat democratic and socialist ideas with the idea of great-power "patriotism," the struggle with "aliens," and so on. To the extent that hopes for the success of the Stolypin agrarian policy died out, nationalism became for tsarism the only means that tsarism relied on to restrain the people from revolution.

The liberals openly embraced chauvinism and nationalism in the period of the June 3 monarchy. P. B. Struve, a member of the Central Committee of the Kadet party, even worked out a nonsensical theory of "creative," "advancing" nationalism. Antisemitism was an expression and index of militant nationalism. In the June 3 monarchy this long-standing official government policy took on racist forms. . .

In March 1911 the Right wing in the Council of State, headed by P. N. Durnovo and V. F. Trepov, unleashed a second "ministerial" crisis against Stolypin, the final result of which was his political and then physical demise. The pretext was a bill on zemstvos [provincial and district institutions of self-government] in the western provinces. Its basic point, the segregation of voters into national curiae, was declared by the rightists to be incompatible with the basic foundations of "Russian statehood" because it supposedly created a precedent by which each non-Russian nationality might claim separate representation, seeking its own interests in direct contradiction to the interests of the Russian Empire as a whole. In actuality this charge was entirely senseless, for the electoral laws of both 1905 and 1907 envisaged elections to the Duma by separate nationalities. On March 4, 1911, the Council of State adopted an amendment rejecting national curiae, which was tantamount to rejection of the whole bill.

In reply Stolypin submitted his resignation, and both the higher-ups and the Duma considered the acceptance of the resignation as a settled matter. But at the last moment it turned out that Stolypin was staying in power on the basis of conditions that he proposed and the tsar accepted: Durnovo and Trepov were sent away "on leave" until January 1, 1912; both legislative chambers were dismissed for three days so that the bill could be passed under article 87 [providing for the passage of decrees when the legislative bodies were not in session].

It appeared that Stolypin had gained complete victory, but this was not so in actuality. Everyone understood that his political career was finished. . . .He himself told Kokovtsov, his future successor, that his days as premier were numbered, that "they are getting at him from all sides," that he "will not be here for long." One of the reasons for the temporary retention of Stolypin was that the tsar did not wish to create a "constitutional" precedent — the acceptance of the resignation of the head of a government as a result of his conflict with "representative" institutions. Therefore it was decided to remove him quietly, finding him some sort of honorific post far from the real center of power. However, the *okhranka* [secret police] had the last word. On September 1, 1911, Stolypin was fatally wounded by Bogrov, an agent of the *okhranka,* and died several days later. Thus the career of the would-be Russian Bismarck came to its inglorious end. . . .

While recognizing the failure of the Stolypin course, tsarism was obliged to adhere to it right to the end of its existence, for there was no other way open. This was the inescapable situation of reaction, the historic destiny of the rotten regime.

Peter Stolypin's grave in Kiev is marked by a simple black slab from which the metal letters have been wrenched, but even Soviet tourist guides sometimes point it out with a touch of awe. Stolypin was a man who could compel some kind of respect even from his enemies. Among historians, his staunchest supporter was LEONID I. STRAKHOVSKY (1898–1963), who did not live to complete his full-scale biography of the premier. Strakhovsky's father, like Stolypin, was a provincial governor, and the two men were on good terms. After the revolution Strakhovsky lived for many years in the United States and Canada, writing a biography of Alexander I and a study of the allied intervention in northern Russia during the Civil War and editing a widely used *Handbook of Slavic Studies*. He held appointments at Harvard University, Georgetown University, the University of Maryland, and the University of Toronto. Both Strakhovsky and Miliukov hold that the best opportunities for collaboration between the Duma and the government were missed. How do they differ in assigning responsibility for this failure?*

Leonid I. Strakhovsky

Stolypin's Progressive Statesmanship

[Stolypin's] success in dealing with the Duma [while he was minister of internal affairs] prompted the tsar to appoint him prime minister on 8 July 1906, while he still retained the post of minister of internal affairs. It was the tsar's personal decision, and it came as a complete surprise not only to Stolypin but also to Goremykin, whom he was to replace as head of the government. To complicate matters, the tsar had decided to dissolve the Duma when announcing the change of government. Stolypin definitely dissociated himself from the reactionaries who surrounded the throne, yet he had no choice but to accept his sovereign's command. However, at an audience with the tsar on 10 July 1906, he stated two conditions upon which he would accept the premiership: first, the immediate dismissal of two ministers who had made themselves conspicuously odious by their reactionary tendencies and a free hand for a further reshuffling of the cabinet; second, the eventual formation of a

*From Leonid I. Strakhovsky, "The Statesmanship of Peter Stolypin," *Slavonic and East European Review*, vol. 37, no. 89 (London, June 1959), pp. 351–354, 356–364, 366–368, 370. Reprinted with omissions by permission of the editors of the *Slavonic and East European Review*, the School of Slavonic and East European Studies, London.

coalition government which was to include members of the opposition. The tsar granted these conditions and noted in his diary: "I received Stolypin; from his first steps I obtained the best impression."

Stolypin faced an extremely tense situation. The day before he assumed office the first Duma was dissolved and the date for the convocation of the second Duma was fixed for 15 March 1907. This gave the government two hundred days in which to pacify the country by combating terrorism and introducing much-needed reform. The task was complicated not only by the revolutionary parties which were preparing another uprising, but also by the liberal constitutional democratic party which had the largest single representation in the first Duma. Its leaders went to Finland and from Vyborg issued an appeal to the Russian people claiming that the dissolution of the Duma was illegal and exhorting them to resist the government by refusing to pay taxes or to be inducted into the armed forces. Contrary to expectations Stolypin permitted the signatories of the Vyborg manifesto to return home. However, they were indicted and eventually condemned for an attempt to stir up revolt. During the trial which lasted from 12 to 18 December 1906, 166 of them were found guilty and condemned to three months' imprisonment. But while under indictment, they lost their right to stand for election to the second Duma.

Notwithstanding this opposition from the leaders of the constitutional democratic party who had previouly aligned themselves with the revolutionary parties in the first Duma, Stolypin tried to obtain their collaboration, together with that of the octobrists, for a coalition government. But he found insurmountable difficulties from the start. S. A. Muromtsev, president of the first Duma and a leading light of the con-

stitutional democratic party, declined the offer of collaboration, explaining:

Revolutionary outbreaks, against which the government would be forced to take severe repressive measures, are inevitable; this in turn will undoubtedly arouse discontent in public circles and thus deprive the government of the needed support on the part of the public.

P. N. Miliukov, leader of the constitutional democratic party, refused all collaboration with and support of a coalition government, demanding a cabinet of members of his own party, the largest party in the first Duma, with himself as prime minister. "Such a cabinet was immediately to enact the constitutional democratic party's programme of expropriation of land, general political amnesty, abolition of courts martial, and the convocation of a constituent assembly to decide the future form of government, i.e., the retention of a limited monarchy or the establishment of a republic." Needless to say, Stolypin could not accept these demands, first because he was entrusted with power by the tsar and authorised only to form a coalition government and not to surrender this power, and secondly because he believed in the principle and institutions of monarchy and merely wanted to transform Russia's unlimited autocracy into a constitutional monarchy of the Western type.

Having thus failed to enlist the collaboration of the constitutional democrats, he turned to the octobrists, i.e. the supporters of the manifesto of 17 October 1905 which established a constitutional régime in Russia. . . . On 28 July 1906, he invited [the liberals] Shipov and Prince Lvov to join his cabinet, but they both declined. Two days later in a letter to Stolypin and speaking for his whole group, Shipov wrote:

We propose that out of thirteen cabinet posts, besides that of the prime minister, not less than seven should be given to persons representing the public . . . these would hold the portfolios of internal affairs, justice, public instruction, agriculture, commerce, high procurator of the Holy Synod and state comptroller.

This, of course, would have meant the surrender of power to the opposition, which Stolypin could not accept. In a reply to Shipov, dated the same day, he wrote:

I am very vexed that I was not able to express to you my point of view clearly enough and that I left with you the impression that I am a person who is afraid of bold reforms and who is a partisan of "small concessions." The fact is that I do not recognise any concessions, either big or small. I believe that real action, real reforms are necessary and that we must, in the interval of 200 days which separate us from the convocation of a new Duma, devote ourselves entirely to the preparation and to the enactment of what is possible. Such "action" will speak more than the strongest words.

Although recognising his failure to enlist public men in his government, Stolypin did not want to alienate the liberal opposition altogether. Since news about his negotiations had leaked out and rumours and speculations were spreading widely, he issued an official statement to the press on 27 July in which he declared that "the desire of the government to bring public men of the opposition into the cabinet . . . met with difficulties which arose despite the good will of the government and of the public men themselves." Although a radical writer later characterised the words of this conciliatory statement as "sheer and unequivocal truth," the "public men" responded with a letter to the press claiming that the official statement was untrue since the negotiations had broken down because "the conditions laid down by us were not accepted by the prime minister." And Count Heyden remarked cynically to Shipov: "Apparently we were being in-

vited to play the role of hired children to accompany ladies of easy virtue." Thus ended Stolypin's "*bona fide* attempt" to enlist public men as members of his cabinet in order to work together for the good of the country. Although later, in the third Duma, he was able to rely on the support of the Octobrists, the Constitutional Democrats remained His Majesty's "disloyal" opposition and worked steadily hand-in-hand with the revolutionary parties not only against the government but also against Stolypin personally. History has shown how short-sighted and narrow-minded they were. . . .

During his five years in office he was the most hunted man in Russia. And while as a person he could face danger with courage and equanimity, as the head of the government he had to act boldly and decisively to stem the spread of revolutionary terror. This terror was directed not only against the high officials of the government, the court, the army and navy, but also against the rank and file of government employees, officers, and even ordinary policemen. Thus, from November 1905 to June 1906, from among the employees of the ministry of the interior alone 288 persons were killed and 383 wounded, while 156 others were attacked but escaped injury. Up to the end of October 1906 a total of 3,611 government officials of all ranks had been killed or wounded. The need for stern measures was pressing. This was realised by the tsar himself, who sent a message to Stolypin on 14 August 1906: "I command the council of ministers to inform me without delay what measures it considers most adequate to undertake in order to carry out my immovable will to uproot rebellion and to re-establish order." To this he added in a postscript: "It seems that only an extraordinary law, promulgated as a temporary measure until peace and quiet are re-established, could give assurance that the government had undertaken decisive measures and would thus quiet everyone."

In fulfilment of this command, Stolypin enacted on 19 August with the approval of his entire cabinet, the establishment of field courts martial and gave discretionary powers to governors-general to have terrorists tried by military courts, often without due process of law. All told, from the day of their institution until their abolition on 20 April 1907, these field courts martial sentenced to death and had executed 1,144 persons. In addition, 329 persons were sentenced to hard labour, 443 to imprisonment for different lengths of time, and 7 to exile, while 71 were acquitted. The law establishing them was promulgated under article 87 of the fundamental laws which gave the government the right to enact legislation in the interval between Duma sessions subject to approval by the next Duma. It was permitted to lapse, because the government did not present it for the approval of the second Duma since it was certain of rejection. But terrorist activity continued long after the abolition of field courts martial, through it slackened after 1907. . . .

In a government declaration of 24 August 1906, Stolypin justified the use of article 87 not only for the establishment of field courts martial but also for the enactment of much-needed reforms. All told in the interval between the first and second Dumas, he enacted 59 important laws under the authority of article 87. Interestingly enough he received support for all these actions from A. I. Guchkov, leader of the Octobrists, who had refused to enter his cabinet and who now declared in an interview:

I have absolute confidence in Stolypin; until now we have not had such talented and capable persons as he at the seat of power. I am convinced that he will apply all his efforts for the realisation of his programme. I believe in the purity of his intentions and in his ardent love for our poor martyred fatherland, but everything will depend on the extent of his authority. The fulfilment of the promises which he has made in his declaration will be possible only if he has sufficient power to carry them out.

For the time being at least Stolypin had the confidence and support of the tsar, hence the power to carry out his programme.

As a preliminary measure to his far-reaching land reform, Stolypin obtained the consent of the tsar for the transfer of appanage lands to the peasant land bank for sale among the land-short peasants. This was enacted on 12 August 1906, the very day he almost became the victim of revolutionary terrorists. On 27 August state lands were added to the funds of the peasant land bank. On 5 October, a decree abolished the last vestiges of serfdom: the peasants were equalised with other classes in their rights and became eligible for offices in the local administration, some of which were made elective. Also they could no longer be punished by land captains without trial. Finally, on 9 November 1906, Stolypin enacted his famous agrarian law which followed his fundamental idea of liberating the individual peasant from the stranglehold of the village commune. . . .

When defending his agrarian law later in the second Duma, Stolypin pointed out that if all the land of whatever kind was divided among the peasants, each peasant household would possess in the fourteen central provinces of European Russia less than forty acres and in some provinces only twenty-one. Futhermore, the increase of population among the peasants in European Russia alone amounted to 1,625,000 a year, which would necessitate the provision yearly of nine and a half million acres if each newcomer was to have an average-sized holding; but there were no such reserves of land in Russia. Hence Stolypin's agrarian law backed the thrifty and industrious peasant by offering to him new opportunities and the right to own his land, and took it for granted that the lazy and indolent elements in the peasant class would either be eliminated altogether or driven into the ranks of urban workers, since the growing industries of Russia demanded more and more labour. This process of transforming peasants into urban workers was already then quite far advanced.

The law of 9 November tackled practically every aspect of the agrarian problem. It set out in the first instance to improve the conditions of peasant farming by the substitution of compact enclosed freehold farms for the existing medley of agricultural units held communally by the village. It also provided for the improvement of the system of tenure on lands remaining in communal ownership by helping the peasants to eliminate inconveniences caused by the jumbling together of lands assigned to different individuals. It included the provision of technical and financial assistance to peasant farmers for the improvement of their holdings and cultivation. Through the peasant land bank, whose statute was revised so as to enable it greatly to extend its operations, mainly for the benefit of the poorer peasantry, Stolypin's agrarian law helped the peasants to buy more land on liberal conditions of credit, thus inaugurating a scheme of widespread internal colonisation. Last, but not least, it opened up Asiatic Russia to surplus population by developing a system of assisted migration on a large scale into the south-eastern steppes and organising the colonisation of Siberia. . . .

[After passing the Duma on 24 April 1909, the agrarian reform law] was passed by the council of state and on 14 June 1910 it was signed by the tsar. It was incorporated in the code of laws as the statute for land settlement on 29 May 1911, and thus became one of the fundamental laws.

These dates show clearly what a long battle Stolypin had to wage for his agrarian reform. But the results were encouraging. By the time of the enactment of the law, over two and a half million heads of families had given formal notification of their desire to leave the commune; and by the end of 1914 nearly two million heads of families enjoyed private land-ownership, while an additional half-million had received certificates entitling them to ownership of their communal lots in villages where there had not been a redistribution of land for the last twenty years. All told, this represented over 25 per cent of peasants in village communes. . . .

The opening of the second Duma was fixed for 20 February 1907. In order not to repeat the error of the preceding government and let the new assembly waste its time in sterile declamations, Stolypin had prepared a vast legislative programme. In addition to the agrarian law, it included legislation concerning religious liberty, *habeas corpus,* civic equality, state insurance for the benefit of the working classes, an income tax bill, reform of the *zemstva,* establishment of *zemstva* in the Baltic provinces and Poland where they did not then exist, and reform of local tribunals, of higher and secondary schools, and of the police. But the Duma was in an ugly mood. At the opening session, during the reading of the imperial decree calling it into being, the whole left including the constitutional democrats remained seated. This was meant to be an expression of their opposition, but actually, of course, was merely bad manners.

On 6 March, two weeks after the second Duma opened, Stolypin read the government declaration outlining his entire programme for the immediate future. He was followed on the tribune by Tseretelli, a menshevik, who delivered a fiery speech, which was an outright appeal for revolution, full of hatred toward the government and constituted authority. Other orators from the left added their bit to the fire, while the protests of the right transformed the meeting into bedlam, which was quieted only by a recess. After the Duma reconvened, Stolypin demanded to be heard. He was a born orator; the historic speech he delivered had not been prepared. It was brief but breathed such force and such dignity that no disrespectful shout was heard during its delivery. After stating that the government would like to find a common ground and language with the Duma and that there was no place for hatred in common work, he ended with these words:

All these attacks are intended to cause a paralysis of will and thought in the government and the executive; they can be summed up in two words addressed to the authorities: "Hands up!" To these words, gentlemen, the government, confident in its righteousness, can answer calmly with only two other words: "Not afraid!"

This speech made a tremendous impression. People felt that here was a real man at the head of the government. But the majority of the second Duma refused Stolypin's proffered hand. . . .

On 3 June 1907 the second Duma was dissolved and simultaneously an imperial decree announced a new electoral law and set 1 November as the date for the convocation of the third Duma. This electoral law, the opposition claimed, was in violation of the fundamental laws, but it resulted in creating a working majority in the third Duma which was willing to and did co-operate with the government. . . .

During the time of the third Duma, Stolypin had only one major setback and it came from the right but not in the Duma. On 4 March 1910 the council of state, led by a bloc of reactionary landowners, voted down a law for the introduction of *zemstva* in Poland which had been previously passed by the Duma. This action sought to avoid the imposition of heavier taxes on large estates and to prevent the development of progressive and liberal ideas which thrived in these autonomous bodies, as experience in other parts of Russia had proved. The day after this rejection of one of his major reforms by the upper chamber, Stolypin tendered his resignation to the tsar.

At first the tsar seemed inclined to accept the resignation of his prime minister; but the energetic intervention of his cousins, Grand Dukes Nicholas Mikhailovich and Alexander Mikhailovich, the latter being also his brother-in-law because he was married to the tsar's sister Xenia, and finally that of his mother, led him to change his mind. [Therefore Nicholas II asked Stolypin to remain in office and promised the premier his cooperation.]. . .

Stolypin complied with the tsar's request, but consented to remain as head of the government only on condition that, first, the Duma and the council of state should immediately be prorogued for three days so that he could put into effect the introduction of *zemstva* in Poland under the provision of article 87 and, secondly, that the two leaders of the right-wing opposition in the council of state—Durnovo and Trepov—be sent on leave of absence until the end of the year. The tsar agreed to these demands of his prime minister, but not satisfied with an oral promise, Stolypin requested that the sovereign should write these conditions down, which Nicholas II did in his own hand in blue pencil on a large sheet of paper. . . .

Consequently on 12 March 1910 the legislative chambers were prorogued for three days, during which the law establishing *zemstva* in Poland was promulgated under article 87. Both the Duma, which had adopted the law, and the council of state, which had rejected it, were incensed at this high-handedness on Stolypin's part. They demonstrated their opposition to the prime minister at Durnovo's departure abroad, when at the railway station almost all members of the council of state and many members of the Duma of all political parties participated in an imposing farewell.

Stolypin was the victor, but it was a Pyrrhic victory. He alienated the Duma, which feared that the disregard of the constitutional prerogatives of the council of state could be also applied to it at some time. Needless to say, he alienated the council of state where even moderate members now looked on him with suspicion and enmity. Finally, the tsar never forgave Stolypin the distrust shown in his word when Stolypin requested a written confirmation of the sovereign's consent. "Perhaps in this case Stolypin was right," wrote Shidlovsky, "but tsars never forgive such distrust." Hence hereafter Stolypin could not work as before with the three sources of power in the country: the tsar, the Duma, and the council of state. . . .

An assassin's bullet stopped Stolypin's useful activity. After his death his work, particularly in the agrarian field, was not continued with the same vigour, and finally Russia was plunged into war long before she had recovered internally. "And what more propitious circumstances for trouble could be created than by war!" Stolypin had exclaimed in 1909. Even though he made mistakes, his personality, his courage, his liberal ideas, and progressive statesmanship remain permanently inscribed in the annals of history.

One of the older generation of Soviet historians who survived the vicissitudes of the Stalin years with unimpaired scholarly vigor is S. M. DUBROVSKY (b. 1900). A member of the Institute of History of the Academy of Sciences, he is the author of numerous books and articles on agrarian history, including *The Stolypin Land Reform* (1963), which some Western specialists in Russian history regard as the best Soviet work dealing with the twentieth century, based on extensive archival research. Considering Dubrovsky's mastery of the source material, it may seem irritating and superfluous for him to introduce Lenin's opinion at all the key junctures. One must, however, bear in mind that Lenin devoted a great deal of time to study of the economics of Russian agriculture before World War I. While his political zeal colored his interpretation, Lenin's analysis of the Russian agrarian scene was not merely unfounded propaganda.*

S. M. Dubrovsky

Stolypin Against the Peasants

The fate of the democratic revolution in Russia depended directly on the success or failure of the Stolypin reform, which undoubtedly had some chance of succeeding.

The Stolypin reconstruction of the countryside might have been able to defer the necessity of a bourgeois revolution among the peasantry "if the Stolypin agrarian policy had lasted a very, very long time, if it had definitely reconstructed all rural land relationships on a purely bourgeois pattern." "In history," wrote Lenin, "there have been examples of the *success* of such a policy. It would be empty, silly democratic phraseology if we said that in Russia the success of such a policy is 'impossible.' It is possible!"

If the Stolypin reform had destroyed the remnants of serfdom in the process of the development of capitalism on the Prussian model [large, capitalist farms employing hired labor], this would have reduced the prospects of a peasant democratic revolution. But this does not mean that in general there would have been no possibility of revolution in the countryside. Should Stolypin have won out, the prospects of a socialist revolution would still have remained, based on the agricultural proletariat in the countryside and the poor peasants, the middle peasants having been neutralized. . . .

The government realized very clearly that it was struggling to liquidate peasant revolution when it carried out the agrarian

*From S. M. Dubrovsky, *Stolypinskaia zemel'naia reforma (The Stolypin Land Reform)* (Moscow: Institute of History of the Academy of Sciences, 1963), pp. 61, 63, 162, 164, 187–188, 305–306, 568–569. Translated by Robert H. McNeal.

reform. Therefore it adopted violent measures in its relations with the main mass of the peasantry, aiming at the complete success of its reform. In allocating all its resources to the capitalist reformation of the countryside, the government was making its last cast of the dice; it was opening the "last valve" (Lenin). This was the final effort to postpone the demise of the old order. The fate of the revolution in Russia depended on the success or failure of the reform. "The definitive transition of the tsar's government, the landlords and rich bourgeoisie (Octobrists) to the new agrarian policy," wrote V. I. Lenin, "has great historical significance. The fate of bourgeois revolution in Russia — not only the present revolution, but the possibilities for further democratic revolution — depends *most of all* on the success or failure of this policy. . . ."

The tsar's government, convinced that the execution of the projected reform would prevent a new peasant uprising, concentrated all the strength and might of the state to achieve the forcible realization of the legislative acts that it had devised. The ministry of internal affairs, including the police department, played the largest role in preserving and strengthening the dictatorship of the feudal landlords. In particular this ministry was in charge of all the affairs of the nobility, their assemblies, expenses for the support of the ruling estate, and so on. The Social Democrat Belousov, when the Duma was considering the budget of the ministry of internal affairs in 1909, was basically correct when he said that estimates of the ministry represented the nobility's private treasury. At the same time, the ministry of internal affairs was in charge of the entire administrative system of the peasant estate. It played the leading role in the conduct of land reform, even though its concerns were far removed from agronomical or agricultural considerations. In 1906–1911 "Stoly-

pin himself" headed the ministry of internal affairs, while he was also chairman of the council of ministers (premier), thus concentrating vast power in his hands. The police department and all the central administrative-police power was in the hands of this ministry, giving it great power and authority among all the other branches of the tsarist government. The ministry of internal affairs organized the land reform through its land section, which headed the administration of all peasant affairs in the country.

The main figure in the actual rearrangement of landholding in the Stolypin reform was not the agronomist but the *zemskii nachal'nik* [land captain], who was usually one of the local nobility, or a person with close ties to the nobility. The police-administrative tasks of the reform took priority in comparison to other tasks, agricultural ones in particular. Administratively Russia was divided into provinces, the provinces into districts. All the districts were divided into territories assigned to land captains, of which there were more than 2,500 at the time of the Stolypin reform. These land captains constituted a feudal landlord dictatorship on the countryside, a regime of the 30,000 landlords who actually ran the whole government. . . .

The government's coercive measures were not at all decisive in the real development of agriculture and relationships on the land. Coercion was only the midwife of growing capitalism in an agricultural economy on the Prussian model. The degree to which the projected government measures were realized depended directly on the level of economic development which was attained in rural Russia in the period between the two revolutions [1905 and 1917] and on the course of the class struggle. In actuality, what was the basic content of the reform that we are considering? It was the destruction of the commune, the creation of *khutors* [farms on consolidated parcels of land, on which the peasant lived] and *otrubs* [farms on consolidated parcels of land, the peasant's house remaining in a village], the resettlement, mainly in the East, of part of the peasantry, and the decontrol of purchase and sale of land. The commune often had been regarded as a necessary form of organization of the peasantry, as long as self-sufficient, non-intensive agriculture was the rule, with common pasturage of cattle, and as long as the countryside retained significant remnants of the semiserf order. As is known, the three-field system was rather widespread in such feudal agriculture. The development of capitalism in agriculture made possible the replacement of the three-field rotation of crops, the improvement of animal husbandry and soil cultivation, the specialization of agriculture, the division of labor, and so on. In the period under consideration the more prosperous peasants changed from the commune to other forms of landholding, in particular the *khutor* and *otrub*, in proportion to the development of capitalism and the disintegration of serfdom. The prosperous peasants began to improve their farming only when there were favorable conditions. Under capitalism the desire for improved farming, the break-up of the three-field system and the introduction of the multifield system, the change from communal to private land tenure, grows only when the market offers a large demand for agricultural products and the prosperous peasants have accumulated the necessary capital to support more advanced agriculture. Thus, the outcome reform was dependent on the success of the transition to the Prussian model of agriculture, which was taking place in Russia, and on the social stratification of the countryside and the development of the class struggle there.

There was no revolution in the economy of rural Russia between 1905 and 1917.

There was only a tendency toward improved farming among the prosperous peasants and the further development of capitalism on the Prussian model. And this trend toward agricultural improvement on capitalist lines, which varied among regions, predetermined the relative success of the Stolypin land system in one place and its failure in others. The old communal land tenure disintegrated to the extent that the countryside, represented by its more prosperous strata, changed over to capitalist farming in a given region. But since capitalist improvement in agriculture was far from embracing even the upper levels of the peasantry and these improvements appeared in different regions with unequal force, the reform did not yield the results which the government expected from it. Most important, the process of the implementation of the Stolypin land reform greatly intensified the revolutionary struggle in the countryside. In the end a new democratic revolution triumphed in the countryside, passing directly on to the proletarian socialist revolution. . . .

In its land policy the tsarist government tried by all the means at its disposal to direct the development of the country on the Prussian pattern. But this effort suffered complete failure. First, even the quantitative results were insignificant. As the result of ten years of land reform only 10 percent of all peasant farms were made into *khutors* or *otrubs*. The objective significance of this 10 percent was exceedingly small. In the Stolypin years there already appeared a tendency toward the destruction of separate farms that had been established, namely the threatened splitting up of *khutors* and *otrubs* as families partitioned their land among their members. To a considerable extent this would make the Stolypin land reform ineffectual. The government was even attempting to work out a way of limiting the partition of *khutors* and *otrubs* through restriction or prohibition of the partition of the family's land, introducing what amounted to a limitation of inheritance to one heir only.

The conditions for the development of separate farms were completely unfavorable. Remnants of serfdom, the poor development of the market, and the general economic backwardness of the country retarded the development of *khutors* and *otrubs* that the government encouraged. The general result was that only a small portion of the *khutors* and *otrubs,* which were owned by kulaks, who had lived prosperously even before the reform, were able to develop their farms. The mass of peasants who were not prosperous took up a *khutor* from necessity, because the Stolypin reform left them no alternative, and became still poorer. " 'When you've no place to go, go to a *khutor*,' say these peasants. Starving and suffering on beggarly farms, they grasp at straws, whether grants to migrate east, or loans to put their affairs in order. They struggle with the *khutors* as fish against ice; they sell all their grain in order to pay a bank loan; they are constantly in debt; they live in shocking poverty; they live like paupers; they are *driven off* the *khutors* for *defaulting loans* and they are transformed into homeless beggars" [wrote Lenin in 1913].

An especially hard lot was that of the middle peasants, who, flattered by the long-term credit offered them by the "peasants' " (actually landlords') bank, bought land with the assistance of the bank and became indebted beyond their means. . . .

Thus Stolypin's wager on the *khutor* and *otrub* failed. The "progress" of *khutors* and *otrubs* was insignificant. Stolypin did not even attain a revolution in the conditions of kulak farms. He did not achieve any important change in the situation of the rest of the farms. Nine-tenths of them continued to work their land in strips. Agricultural conditions became even worse, because strip farming formerly could be slightly ameliorated by communal redistribution of the strips among families. Now that was impossible. The former means of regulating land use was to a considerable extent destroyed, and new means had not as yet been fully developed. In such conditions land reform often confused land tenure more than before. In general there was disorganization rather than reorganization of land tenure.

One must take into account also that very soon *khutors* and *otrubs* were actually being destroyed, both by the process of concentration of the land into large farms and the process of the partition of small farms. The peasantry, which was in the main ill-disposed toward the Stolypin land program, actually strove to destroy its results by carrying on repartition of the land. . . .

The Prussian model of agricultural development in Russia was a fiasco. As early as the period of the Stolypin regime V. I. Lenin emphasized that "over this 'great reform' wafts the odor of death." The development of the class struggle, the growth of the workers' revolutionary movement, the rise of the revolutionary struggle on the countryside brought the Stolypin government and the entire old regime in Russia more and more rapidly to its demise under the blows of revolution. In contradiction to the opinion of the opportunists, the "Stolypin reform" did not eliminate the necessity of revolution but made it inevitable. The role of the peasantry in it not only failed to diminish, but grew all the more. "The more the tsar and the Duma," wrote V. I. Lenin, "help the rich peasants to ravage the peasant mass, the more conscious this mass becomes, the less it retains its faith in the tsar, the faith of bond slaves, the faith of oppressed and unenlightened people. With each year the rural [wage] laborer becomes more numerous in the countryside — for him there is no place to seek salvation except in union with the urban worker for the common struggle. With each year there are more ruined, completely impoverished, starving peasants—from them millions and millions will come forth, when the urban proletariat arises in more decisive, more unified struggle with the tsar and landlords." The February and then the Great October Socialist Revolution testified to the correctness of Ilyich's prevision.

Nikolai Gogol's satirical play *The Inspector General* pretty well sums up the popular image of the bureaucracy of imperial Russia: venal, stupid, immobile. Most liberal and socialist historians in Russia and the West have accepted this image, usually without skepticism or detailed investigation. Recently, however, GEORGE L. YANEY (b. 1930), a professor of history at the University of Maryland, took up this topic without such traditional preconceptions. He wrote a doctoral dissertation, as yet unpublished, on the Stolypin land reform, and has broadened his perspective in articles on three key ministries of the imperial government, the writings of Korkunov, who was an expert on Russian law, and some of the problems of political theory which are embodied in the history of the Russian state. Yaney is far from denying that Russia faced serious problems between 1905 and 1914, but his appraisal of the competence of the bureaucracy suggests that it was not a foregone conclusion that the regime was incompetent in coping with them.*

George L. Yaney

Constructive Governmental Action Among the Peasantry

In the conventional view of the [Stolypin land] Reform, it is assumed that the tsar's ministers devised it in 1905–6 and that its subsequent execution was simply a matter of carrying out their initial decisions. But the Reform actually developed as a continuing experiment. The enabling decrees chiefly those of November 3, 1905, March 4, 1906, and November 9, 1906, were hypotheses to be tested rather than the sole basis for the Reform's development, and the carrying out of the Reform was more a process of trial and error than the execution of a preconceived plan. In 1905–6, the tsar's ministers did not know what programs would be suitable to their ultimate purpose, and they had no reliable way of discovering such programs save by observing the results of what their executive agencies did. The early decrees were almost entirely couched in vague and general terms, and the few specific instructions in them were tentative. They suggested a number of possible courses of action and allowed the local commissions of the Reform organization to undertake whichever ones they found suitable to their respective areas. As the commissions began to operate, the central organization of the Reform (the Chief Committee for Land

*From George L. Yaney, "The Concept of the Stolypin Land Reform," *Slavic Review,* vol. 23, no. 2 (June 1964), pp. 275–279, 282–293. By permission of the editors and the author.

Settlement) learned from their experience which programs were enjoying the greatest success. Within a few years the government began to de-emphasize the programs that had originally been thought to be important and concentrated its main efforts on the ones which worked best in practice.

The Reform's enactors were aware in 1906 that they were experimenting. A. V. Krivoshein, who was the minister of agriculture and executive director of the Reform from 1908 to 1915 and also the author of the decree which set up the Reform organization, freely admitted that he did not know what the Reform's main programs would be. In a memorandum of February, 1906, to Nicholas II, he said: "It is important to act; we must begin and our very acting will show us the best ways to accomplish our purpose." Accordingly, Krivoshein set up the Reform organization to operate as a service agency without statutory power. The local commissions could carry out only those programs which they could persuade the peasants to accept. The commissions' actual accomplishments, then, developed out of their interaction and negotiation with the peasants and did not simply emerge out of instructions from St. Petersburg. It was the experience of this interaction, more than any other factor, which produced the changes in the government's programs that occurred after 1906. What is now remembered as the Stolypin Land Reform emerged not from legislative enactments or high level policy decisions but rather from the executive operation of the government administration as a whole.

Many writers have asserted that the Reform was essentially a makeshift, enacted in hasty, ill-informed desperation in order to head off a general upheaval among the peasantry. S. Iu. Witte, who before 1905 had been the government's leading advocate of agrarian reform, expressed this

view in the years after 1906. One might conclude from this that the vague wording of the Reform decrees, the wide latitude allowed to the local commissions, and the Reform organization's changes of policy after 1906 only demonstrate more clearly the Reform's makeshift nature and the characteristic inability of the tsarist government to control its own administrative organs.

But the Reform was not a poorly devised makeshift carried out in a slipshod fashion any more than it was the simple fulfillment of a preconceived plan. Witte's words after 1906 contradict his own earlier policies. In early 1906 he was, at least for a time, as anxious as anyone to enact land and legal reforms. In all likelihood, his later disapproval of the Reform reflects his personal bitterness at his dismissal from the government which occurred in April, 1906, just as Stolypin was arriving in St. Petersburg to take over what Witte felt was his own creation. Moreover, it is simply not true that the Reform began to materialize only in 1905 under the threat of revolution. The tsarist government's active concern for peasant problems had been growing steadily since 1880, and a number of officials had been getting firsthand experience at working with the peasants. In 1902, some of the leading statesmen embarked on a major effort to develop specific programs of peasant reform. Witte, then the minister of finance, conducted a massive investigation of the peasantry in 1902–4. At about the same time V. I. Gurko, head of the Land Section in the Ministry of Internal Affairs, was drafting a detailed plan of reform. Both Witte's and Gurko's recommendations were very similar to what was finally enacted in 1906. Gurko was himself the author of the November 9, 1906, decree.

There is no doubt that the authors were hurried. Early in 1906 the leading tsarist officials anticipated large-scale peasant violence, and the Reform decrees were de-signed to head it off. Fear of revolution led the Reform's enactors to disguise their intentions. But the substantive programs in the Reform represented much more than the desperate expedients of frightened men striking out at random. They had been in the planning stages for years. Nor can it be maintained that the Reform was primarily a concession to the peasants, although the government apparently wanted everyone to think it was. Before 1907 the peasants gave no sign that they desired any of the programs the Reform decrees proposed. The peasant congresses of 1905 voiced no desire for agrarian reform beyond the distribution of free land, and the peasant representatives in the First and Second Dumas actively opposed the Reform decrees themselves. Thus, if the peasant violence of 1905 had any constructive effect on the government it was only to speed up a process of enactment that had already begun some time before. By 1905 the leading elements in the tsarist government had already come to recognize that the peasants' social and economic development was vital to the state's interest and that the state would have to play an active role in this development. The Reform decrees were vague and tentative, not because the government was frightened into hasty action, but because the problems they were designed to cope with were both complex and unprecedented. No amount of investigation and preparation would have told the government precisely what had to be done. Revolution or no revolution, the executive organization would have to learn by trial and error. . . .

In the beginning the authors of the Reform all agreed that the peasant was not ready for immediate radical land reforms and that it would be many decades before he could develop into a modern farmer. The Reform changed in the years follow-

ing its enactment, because the peasants did in fact accept radical land reform immediately. When large numbers of peasants petitioned for the consolidation of their land into individual plots, the statesmen grew more optimistic. The change in mood called forth changes in the programs that were to be emphasized, and these, it will be seen, changed the very nature of the Reform.

There were actually three Reforms: the one described in the official publications of 1905–6, the one which the enactors really intended to carry out, and the one which finally developed in practice. According to the government's public statements in 1905–6, the purpose of the initial decrees was to facilitate the sale of arable land on easy financial terms to the neediest peasants. But the government's frequent statements that land distribution was its primary objective were not sincere. At best, the Reform's authors intended land sales to the poorest peasants as a small-scale, stopgap relief measure; in fact, most of the land sales that were made in European Russia benefited the wealthier peasants rather than the needy.

None of the statesmen who helped to prepare the Reform believed that additional land would remedy the fundamental ills of the peasant way of life. What they were really trying to do was to set processes in motion which would encourage the peasants to modernize their methods of land use and land division. The statesmen did not believe, however, that the mass of the peasantry was ready for any more than the simplest kind of land reform, and their programs reflected their hesitancy. They anticipated that their ultimate purpose could be achieved only gradually and thought that the best way to begin was to make it possible and even attractive for a peasant head-of-household to claim his share of the hitherto communally owned peasant land as his own personal property; that is, to carry out a purely paper transaction that would have no effect on the peasants' confused system of land division. But legal transfer of title was at best only the first step toward real reform. It was a relatively simple procedure, and the government agencies already in existence could carry it out. The Reform organization which the March 4 decree established was to go further. The new agencies were to help the most progressive peasant either to sell his share of village land and move to a new plot somewhere else or to obtain a single, integral plot somewhere on the lands belonging to his village in exchange for the strips he held. The latter process came to be termed "personal land settlement" (lichnoe zemleustroistvo), or, more commonly, personal consolidation.

Originally, then, the enactors' real aim was to split off the most advanced peasants (that is, the ones who demonstrated the qualities of economic individualism) and encourage their progress. Ultimately this would compel the peasantry as a whole to follow along. A lengthy, more or less random process of follow-the-leader would gradually make collective ownership and the long outmoded open-field system economically impossible; the traditional peasant social order would at last fall apart, and a modern way of life would emerge out of the wreckage of the old. The most the enactors hoped to accomplish immediately, however, was to bring relief to the poorest peasants by land sales on easy terms and to encourage the rest to acquire personal title to the lands they farmed. In short, land reform was desirable but it was to come gradually as the old communities fell apart. Under no circumstances should the government's moderate aims be jeopardized by pushing the peasants into radical changes which they were not ready to accept.

But neither the stated purpose of the Reform decrees nor the government's real intentions were very close to the objectives that the Reform was to acquire in the years to come. By 1910, the government's most important task had come to be the redividing and rearranging of whole villages at once, consolidating not only the lands of the most progressive but those of every peasant household into privately owned, integral plots. A program of community development replaced the government's original intention to disrupt the old villages.

This is not to say that village land settlement was entirely unforeseen in 1906. All the specific operations that the Reform organization carried out, including village consolidation, had been suggested before the Reform got underway. The March 4 decree itself mentioned a variety of land reform projects for villages; the November 9 decree provided officially for village consolidation. When village consolidation quickly developed into a large-scale operation, therefore, it was not entirely new. Nevertheless, its evolution as the Reform's main aim does represent a significant change in the government's policies and purposes.

In 1907–8 large numbers of peasants began to petition collectively for the consolidation of their villages, and it became unmistakably clear during these years that this was a major trend. Officials on all levels of the Reform organization were taken by surprise. Evidently their surprise was sincere, for the initial enactments had given no indication that their authors considered the consolidation of peasant land by whole villages acting together to be an important program. None of the enactments gave any detailed directions as to how the consolidation was to be effected. No administrative preparations were made in the first years of the Reform that would

indicate that the government had anticipated the peasants' acceptance of this radical land reform. Only in 1909 did the government expand its technical training fa-
cilities in order to meet the rapidly increasing demand for surveyors.

The Reform's original programs—the
sale of new lands to the peasants and the
legal transfer of peasant land from collective ownership to individual—began to fall
off after 1910. Not only did the peasants
lose interest in these operations, judging
from the decreasing rate at which they petitioned for them, but the government itself
was inclined to cut them short. Land sales
dropped as the available lands close to the
existing villages were bought up and it became necessary for the peasants to move
long distances to take advantage of the government's loans. Even more significant
was the falling off of legal transfers of ownership by peasants acting independently
of their villages. Legal transfers, . . . had
originally been the chief practical objective
of the Reform's enactors, but the Reform
organization soon found that these transfers
actually obstructed the achievement of
village consolidation. It became apparent
that individuals who acquired their strips
as private property were likely to oppose a
subsequent village consolidation that
would once again shift them to another
plot of ground. Thus the most advanced
villagers, who might have been the leaders
in bringing about village consolidation,
were coming instead to oppose it, and the
bitterest opponents to collective progress
were often those who had not only acquired their land strips as private property
but who also had consolidated them. The
rate at which individuals consolidated
their lands by themselves did not actually
decline during the Reform's years of
operation, but by 1914 the government
was trying to discourage personal consolidation except in cases where the advan-

tages of setting an example of progress before the peasants outweighed the disadvan-
tages of disrupting the community and turning its ablest members against further
progress.

By 1909, then, the government was encouraging the peasants to achieve consolidation in groups—cooperating among
themselves rather than turning against one
another. The Reform had begun as an attempt to hasten what was assumed to be
the inevitable dissolution of the peasant
communities but had evolved instead into
a means for preserving them by modernizing their economic organization. This does
not imply that government officials actually adopted a new political and social
philosophy after 1906. There is no evidence
that they consciously abandoned one
set of convictions and picked up another.
What changed was their action, not necessarily their thought, and thus the change
must be observed first of all in what the
government was doing.

It is clear that the change in the Reform
did not emerge directly from the peasants'
interests or purposes. In 1906 the peasants
knew no more than the government what
the Reform was to become, and in fact
their general attitude toward the idea of
any government action short of free land
distribution ranged only from indifference
to open hostility. Only a very small number of peasants expressed any desire for
consolidation before the commissions began to operate in late 1906.

Essentially, the Reform's major programs and objectives developed as both the
government's executive organs and the
peasants found them to be workable in
practice. This development involved all
levels of the administration, but it apparently began on the lowest echelon,
where government officials worked directly
with the peasants. The officials who
carried out the Reform in the field were

the surveyors and the land captains. The surveyors drew up the necessary plans for carrying out each land reform project and supervised its execution. When whole villages were involved, the projects normally took two summers to complete. During the whole time, both land captains and surveyors had to maintain the villagers' support, for the peasants concerned had the right to reject the project at any time before it was completed. That the surveyors would concern themselves with the success of their projects was assured by an incentive system which awarded bonuses only for completed projects. The land captain was inclined to be helpful because his superiors in the central government paid close attention to the progress of land reform operations in his district (uchastok). Success in land reform brought the land captains promotions to better jobs and sometimes bonuses from the gubernia administration or the generous travel allowances which the Reform organization allowed its officials. . . .

Communication between the Central Committee and the Reform's field workers was thus established along several lines: direct administrative control through its agents on the land settlement commissions, peasant appeals from commission decisions, and minority opinions from both elected and regular members of the commissions. As a result, a set of regular procedures and technical standards of performance uniform for all European Russia evolved within only a few years. A financial and career incentive system was devised for the field workers which rewarded specific, measurable accomplishment rather than personal influence: an unprecedented achievement for the local levels of imperial administration. In addition to its own organization, the Central Committee could work through the various ministries whose representatives made up its membership to secure the cooperation of their respective subordinates. The surveyors, for example, were under the Ministry of Justice; the land captains and governors were under the Ministry of Internal Affairs. The Committee's policies often came out not only in its own instructions but in separate orders from the ministries as well. In the same way, reports of the Reform's progress reached the Committee through a number of separate administrative channels.

This was the system that enabled the local Reform commissions to communicate the lessons of their experience to the central government. The Central Committee responded to this experience by altering its existing policies and instructions. The Committee did not always approve the local practices that were reported to it, but it did sometimes condone practices that were contrary to its official policies if these practices suited the needs and reactions of the local peasants. Three types of land reform that developed out of the Reform's operation illustrate the effects of the government organization's experience on the Reform's development. These were group land settlement, partial consolidation, and the otruby (integral farms whose owners resided in a central village area rather than on the farm plot itself).

Group land settlement (gruppovnoe zemleustroistvo) was the general term used to cover all land reform operations that fell short of consolidation and left a substantial proportion of the land under collective ownership. There was a great variety of them. The most important were the breakup of large villages into small ones and the consolidation of villages from several separate lots into single, integral areas. The peasants' petitions for various kinds of group land settlement increased in number with each year of the Reform, as did the number of operations completed by the Reform organization. By 1914 the Reform organization was carrying out more group land settlement projects than village consolidations.

But group land settlement is significant to this discussion because of the way it developed, not because of its extent. The number of group projects increased rapidly after 1909, precisely at the same time the central government was pushing village consolidation as the Reform's chief aim; and this increase occurred despite the central government's opposition to it. The Central Committee welcomed those group land settlement projects which were specifically intended to bring the peasants closer to consolidation; but the Committee discouraged group land settlement in general, because it distracted the local commissions from consolidation. Throughout all but the first years of the Reform, the St. Petersburg offices were emitting a constant flow of instructions discouraging the local commissions from taking up their time with group land settlement and urging them to devote more attention to consolidation.

Partial consolidation followed a similar pattern. Partial consolidation was the term used to describe a village consolidation that either left some of the land in common possession or failed to reduce the number of plots belonging to each peasant to a sufficiently low number. The Central Committee consistently disapproved of partial consolidation in no uncertain terms; nevertheless, it flourished throughout the time of the Reform. Moreover, it flourished in those areas, such as the region around Moscow, where the existing conditions of peasant life made it the most practicable, not where the government allowed it by arbitrary decision.

The *otrub* farm also developed against the express wishes of the central government. The Reform organization was committed to the ideal aim of the *khutor*, an integral farm with the peasant's own house

on it. No single goal was more often elaborated and justified by officials on all levels, yet less than one-third of all consolidations resulted in *khutory,* and this fraction showed no signs of increasing as the years went by. The rest of the villages consolidated their fields into integral plots—the *otruby*—but kept their dwellings in one central area. The *otruby,* like partial consolidation, appeared mostly in those areas where the peasants themselves demanded them. The *khutory* flourished almost exclusively in Western Russia where the peasants were generally the most advanced. Of the few *khutory* that formed in the rest of European Russia, most were single households that broke away from their villages by themselves.

The development of group land settlement, partial consolidation, and *otruby* all reflect the characteristic pattern of the Reform's evolution. The central government's official aims and orders served as a framework, itself subject to change, within which the local agencies of the Reform reached workable agreements with the peasants concerning the modernization of their land-holding practices. These agreements were often at variance with what the central government wanted, and their nature varied in accordance with the conditions of peasant life in each area. The Central Committee tolerated departures from its orders but maintained enough control over the Reform's development that it succeeded in getting the peasants to carry out radical changes in their way of life, changes for which the peasants themselves had never before shown any desire or inclination. Both government and peasants learned "by their very action," as Krivoshein had suggested in early 1906.

The concept of the Stolypin Reform as an experiment conflicts with a view that has been often expressed: that the Reform was for the most part forced upon the peasants against their will. It is hardly necessary to suggest that since the government did not foresee the development of village consolidation, it could not very well have forced the peasants into it. For several reasons, however, the contention that illegal coercion was responsible for the Reform's success merits further discussion here. Many scholars still believe it to be true, and it conflicts sharply with the concept presented in this essay. Above all, it has not heretofore been discussed, so far as this writer has seen, except in a partisan or offhand manner.

Illegal coercion was, in fact, exercised by officials in some instances, but there is not enough evidence of this to demonstrate that coercion was characteristic of the Reform organization's operation. In any case, coercion was often a two-way affair in those years. Disputes within the villages over consolidation were not always settled by peaceful discussion, and much of the alleged coercion by the local officials was no doubt directed simply toward maintaining order. Peasants were rioting on a large scale until about 1913, and much of European Russia was under martial law during the entire period. Against this background it is extremely difficult to evaluate the legality, or even the purpose, of individual acts of violence. Evidence for an adequate statistical survey does not exist, and such scattered reports as are available provide no conclusive arguments by themselves. A discussion of specific instances of coercion, therefore, would be fruitless. Fortunately, there are other approaches to the issue.

The argument most often cited to prove that the peasants were forced into consolidation against their will is that most of them reverted to collective ownership in the summer and fall of 1917. The peasants, left on their own after the tsarist government's collapse, are supposed to have forced all the consolidated lots back into communal, open-field strips, indicating clearly—so the argument goes—that the Reform had been forced upon them to begin with.

It will be recalled that the sale of new land to needy peasants was the stated purpose of the Reform decrees, and sales actually did go forward on a rather large scale, although they benefited the wealthier peasants rather than the needy. But much of the newly sold land had been rented to local peasants. In effect, the purchasers, often strangers from outside the area, were depriving the older inhabitants of part of their livelihood. Most of the newcomers bought the land in consolidated lots, and when the vengeful former renters took it back in 1917 this usually meant a reversion to three-field farming. Many of the forced reversions occurred in the lower Volga gubernias, which was where most of the Peasant Bank sales had been made. Many others occurred where individuals had split off singly or in small groups from a village. Of the village consolidations, however, only a small minority seem to have been disturbed by the events of 1917, and there is no record that any of the group land settlement projects were attacked. In any case, there was a healthy recrudescence of village consolidation in the early 1920's, carried out spontaneously by the peasants against the necessarily tacit disapproval of the Soviet government. Indeed, consolidation held sufficient attraction by then that even in the government there was a section of opinion openly favoring its further development. It is clear, then, that the peasants did not break down the Reform's major achievements in the months following the tsarist government's collapse, and the old argument that the Reform was characteristically an act of force is untenable.

To sum up, the Stolypin Reform developed out of the interaction between the tsarist government's executive organization and the peasantry during the years of its implementation. The government's long-range objectives were to bring the Russian peasants into the state's political-legal order as full-fledged citizens and to remove traditional obstacles to the development of modern agriculture. Not knowing exactly how to accomplish this, but feeling compelled to act decisively amidst the turbulence of 1905–6, the leading statesmen set up an organization designed to carry out land reforms in agreement with the peasants. In the course of their work, the local officials of this organization found that the government's long-range purposes would be better served by the peasants' collective action than by separating the most able peasants from their fellows. The officials did not simply ask the peasants what they wanted to do and then respond to their petitions. What occurred between 1906 and 1917 was essentially a series of negotiations and experiments. The officials were trying to find practical ways to work toward the central government's objectives. The peasants were becoming aware that their customary way of life was no longer adequate in Russia's rapidly developing economy and they were deciding what to do about it.

It would be quite as incorrect to ascribe the origin of the Reform wholly to the peasants and local officials as it has been to assume that all the decisions were made in St. Petersburg. Obviously, the negotiations on the operating level were influenced by directives from the Central Committee and were limited by the broad framework that the enactments set up. The point here is that the Reform did not originate in any place at any one time with any one man or group of men, nor did it arise full-blown from any conscious legislative process or from the class interests and intrigues that may have been behind any conscious legislative process. It emerged from the actual operation of an executive administration, an operation involving interaction between peasants and local officials on the one hand and between local officials and high-level statesmen on the other.

In carrying out the Stolypin Reform, the imperial government's executive organization was finding its way. It was responding to the needs of the Russian peasants through the purely administrative processes of an absolutist government without relying on democratic institutions and without benefit of instruction from a conscious public opinion. At least in this instance, the central government was able to respond rapidly and effectively to the experience of its local agencies throughout European Russia without losing its administrative control; this despite the glaring inadequacies in its regular organization before 1905. The government acted, observed the results of its action, and responded to these results. The Russian state, acting in its own interest, discovered by its action a workable arrangement between its own purposes and the interests of the peasantry.

Whatever its defects, the Stolypin land reform was a profusely documented undertaking. Russian officials and private investigators at the time produced a large body of statistical information about it, which, like most such data, is susceptible to various interpretations. Professor W. E. MOSSE (b. 1918), of the University of East Anglia in England, has recently attempted to provide a summary appraisal of the problem in the following essay. Unlike Lenin and some historians who believe that the reform was making substantial progress, Mosse maintains that it had quite a limited impact on life on the countryside. At present he is writing a book on "Russia on the Eve of the Revolutionary Crisis." His earlier works include *Alexander II and the Modernization of Russia* and studies in nineteenth-century diplomacy and the history of German Jewry.*

W. E. Mosse

The Economic Failure of the Land Reform

The impact and potential effects of the agrarian legislation known as the "Stolypin Reform" have remained to this day a matter of controversy. Was Stolypin's agrarian policy, as his admirers maintain, tsarism's last chance of saving itself by means of a "peaceful revolution"? Or was it, as critics have argued then and since, a purely bureaucratic and political *ad hoc* device designed to divert the peasantry from attacking landlords' estates, incapable of solving the Russian peasant problem? Whichever view they adopted, contemporaries showed themselves keenly aware of the importance of the attempt. Lenin, in an oft-quoted passage, wrote:

The Stolypin Constitution . . . and the Stolypin agrarian policy mark a new phase in the breakdown of the old semi-patriarchal and semi-feudal system of tsarism, a new movement towards its transformation into a middle-class monarchy. . . . If this should continue for very long periods of time . . . it might force us to renounce any agrarian program at all. It would be empty and stupid democratic phrase-mongering to say that the success of such a policy in Russia is "impossible." It is possible! If Stolypin's policy is continued . . . then the agrarian structure of Russia will become completely bourgeois, the stronger peasants will acquire almost all the allotments of land, agriculture will become capitalistic, and any "solution" of the agrarian problem—radical or otherwise—will become impossible under capitalism.

Stolypin himself, as is well known, claimed that, given twenty years of undisturbed operation, his policy would transform the

*From W. E. Mosse, "Stolypin's Villages," *Slavonic and East European Review,* vol. 43, no. 101 (London, June 1965), pp. 257–258, 263–264, 268–274. Reprinted with omissions by permission of the editors of the *Slavonic and East European Review,* the School of Slavonic and East European Studies, London.

face of Russia. Bertram D. Wolfe, dramatising the situation, considers that

> Lenin saw the matter as a race with time between Stolypin's reforms and the next upheaval. Should the upheaval be postponed for a couple of decades, the new land measures would so transform the countryside that it would no longer be a revolutionary force . . .[1]

Lenin, in Wolfe's view, came close to losing the race. Indeed it is still widely held—and Lenin's carefully phrased analysis is quoted in support—that, had the war of 1914 not put an end to the application of the Stolypin policy, what Lenin considered a possibility would have, in fact, occurred. The success of the policy of Land Settlement *(zemleustroistvo)* would have transformed Russian agriculture by increasing productivity and creating a prosperous and contented peasantry. A new social foundation would have been created for the traditional institutions of the tsarist state. His agrarian policy, above all, made Stolypin the last significant statesman of tsarist Russia. How far is it possible to maintain this view?

To reach some conclusion about the effectiveness and true significance of Stolypin's agrarian policies, it is necessary to get away from the conventional preoccupation with his intentions (the celebrated *stavka na sil'nykh*—wager on the strong) and with the detailed provisions of the Land Settlement laws (as well as the institutions created for their application) and to concentrate instead on the detailed results achieved. . . .

To assess the real impact of Stolypin's policy, it is necessary, first of all, to examine the rate of its application. Stolypin claimed that it needed twenty years for its success: it operated for only nine. The rate of progress during the years of its operation

throws light on the validity of Stolypin's claim.

Preyer, as a result of his investigations, noted that the maximum rate of applications under the new law was reached early in 1909 after which there occurred a significant slowing down. Basing his conclusions on somewhat different data, Owen in turn considers that the climax of the separation movement fell into the period 1907–10, after which there was a steady decline.

These general conclusions are supported by some detailed statistics. Owen, quoting from Russian sources, gives figures for the numbers of heads of households applying for the private appropriation of *nadel* land as well as of those actually leaving the village commune:

Year	Heads of households requesting appropriation	Heads of households leaving commune
1907*	212,000	48,000
1908	840,000	508,000
1909	650,000	580,000
1910	342,000	342,000
1911	242,000	145,000
1912	152,000	122,000
1913	160,000	135,000
1914	120,000	98,000
1915	36,000	30,000

*incompl.

The Land Settlement Committee in 1916 published figures of the number of individual farmsteads set up. These, reflecting as they do the time-lag between application and surveying operations, show a levelling off rather than an actual decline. The same impression is conveyed by the numbers of surveyors provided for in the budgets of the Committee. There is little doubt that land settlement from 1909 or 1910 onwards was in fact slowing down. It is difficult not to wonder what the rate of its progress would have been in the additional eleven years demanded by Stolypin.

The results achieved by the policy of land settlement were, moreover, by no

---

[1] Bertram D. Wolfe, *Three Who Made a Revolution* (New York, 1949), p. 360.

means uniformly distributed over the 47 provinces involved. When Witte, in March 1910, delivered his final verdict on Stolypin's legislation, he drew attention to the fact that, while some parts of the empire were undoubtedly ripe for the destruction of the commune, many others clearly were not. The bill of 1910, he complained, was

strictly the result of bureaucratic work . . . it pretends to solve one of the most important questions in the life of the Empire by means of sixty articles, and attempts to do it throughout the whole expanse of this huge Empire with one stroke of the pen.

Nothing had been done "to find out where this fruit is ripe and where it is still green, or where it might still be in its embryonic stage." Köföd's survey of the progress of land settlement four years later forms an eloquent commentary on these words. The reform, Köföd noted, had "caught on" in the western and southern provinces of the empire. Elsewhere, it had slowly made some headway

but it is already evident that neither in the Central Agricultural nor in the Industrial regions, neither in the north nor in the south-west will it ever develop with the same vigour as in the southern and south-eastern steppes.

Certain parts of the empire, it is clear, were ripe for the change while others were not. . . .

The evidence . . . clearly indicates that in the central black earth provinces—and it was here that the basic problems of land shortage and rural over-population were most acute and the numbers involved the largest—the policy of land settlement encountered obstacles retarding or even preventing its implementation. The relative failure of the policy in these provinces is indeed so striking as to suggest that it might have taken a century rather than ten or even twenty additional years before

serious inroads could have been made on communal forms of organisation. The resistance to Stolypin's policy among the rank and file of the Russian peasantry was far greater than is sometimes supposed.

In fact, from the start, land settlement and, in particular, secession from the commune, had encountered among the peasantry a great deal of opposition. Köföd, reporting to Stolypin at the end of a tour of inspection, attributed this mainly to the hostility of "vested interests." "It often happens," he wrote,

especially in small settlements, that some kulak shopkeeper, holding in bondage a whole peasant settlement, considers the enclosure programme disadvantageous to himself, fearing not without reason that the peasant, on moving to a *khutor*, will escape his tutelage.

Semyonov, himself a "seceder" in the face of communal hostility (in a village in Moscow province), amplifies the picture. On investigating the situation in neighbouring villages, he found that everywhere the movement for secession was started by "the progressive peasantry," those who were literate, who read and who, in 1905, had taken part in meetings and supported the Peasants' Union. The supporters of the old communal system included the "completely black" (ignorant), the indifferent, the old and a smaller number of "thinking" ones, committed to the doctrines of the left. Another element hostile to secession consisted of those with outside earnings, mainly peasants working in Moscow. These peasant workers did not depend for their living primarily on agriculture and they consistently favoured (largely for material reasons) the preservation of the old communal ways.

In fact, while some peasants stood to gain from the change, many others either expected little advantage or were likely to be the losers. Semyonov, mentally, divided his fellow villagers into three categories: those who, on a separate holding, would increase at least threefold the productivity of their land and labour; those whose output would slightly but not significantly increase; and those who depended entirely on the example and influence of their more energetic fellow villagers for the success of their farming operations. Of 45 peasant householders, Semyonov placed 22, 12 and 11 respectively in the three categories. Only half the households, on this calculation, stood to gain even theoretically from a change involving dislocation and serious inconvenience. In fact, Semyonov makes it clear that, even of the potential beneficiaries, only a fraction actively favoured secession. Nor should it be overlooked that the proportions of the "enlightened" and the "obscurantists," the energetic and the lazy would be very different in a backwoods village in Tambov or Chernigov.

One psychological influence militating against change was that of the peasant women. This is mentioned by both Semyonov and Köföd. The women, understandably, preferred the social life of the village to isolation on a *khutor*. Semyonov gives a graphic description of the bitter opposition to change expressed by the peasant woman Aksiniya: "Here we do everything gaily; there it will not be large strips but a grave." Köföd remarks that this factor operated particularly where the menfolk sought seasonal labour outside the village. In such villages, he notes with regret, separation was impossible.

In addition to such psychological factors, there were the purely economic ones. In many parts of the empire, holdings were too small to make consolidation a practical possibility except for the purpose of selling—and some peasants did not wish to leave the land. Again secession was bitterly opposed by heads of households which grazed a disproportionate number of animals on the communal pastures and over the stubble of the common fields. In many cases the lack of access roads, or wells, of drainage or irrigation, made the idea of life on a separated holding unattractive to those who did not otherwise expect to reap real benefits from the change. It was also argued—Semyonov doubts whether in good faith—that isolated farmsteads were more easily robbed and stood in greater danger in the event of fire. Inequalities in the fertility of the soil made division difficult and controversial. Where the village meeting had any say in the matter, it was, understandably, the poorest and remotest acres which were formed into plots for the seceders. All this was, moreover, reinforced by the fact that many peasants simply did not want to make a change.

In fact, looking at the different factors involved, it is hard to avoid the conclusion that separation was for large numbers of peasants an impossibility and for many more at least a positive disadvantage. Still more, clearly, could see in separation no great advantage for themselves. The entire proceedings of land settlement, mounted with such financial and administrative effort, in all probability benefited at best a minority (Stolypin's "strong ones") of the peasants and, in many parts of the empire not even a substantial one at that. There was some truth in the sombre picture drawn during the Duma debates by Tomilov, a doctrinaire *trudovik* deputy. The new law, he claimed, would bring chaos to the villages while benefiting only the privileged. The bulk of the land would pass into the hands of capitalists and of a new brand of "*pomeshchik* (landlord) peasants." This would happen at the expense of the commune. Those deprived of land would join the ranks of the landless proletariat. Some would become farm hands, others move to the cities to increase unemployment there and cause prices to rise. Nor, in view of what had happened at least in the Baltic provinces, did this seem a wholly fanciful picture.

Taking all these adverse factors in conjunction, it is hardly to be wondered at that in many villages secession was bitterly resisted. . . . The "climate of opinion" and "social pressures" in the majority of Russian villages were against the "separators" (backed by the authorities) and in favour of preserving the traditional village commune. At least in the Great Russian portions of the empire Stolypin's reform, far from being welcomed with joy, ran counter to dominant peasant sentiment. It was this, above all, which reduced its chances of success. The passive—and not always passive—resistance of the peasantry in many parts of the empire doomed the policy to comparative failure.

Indeed the separation—in over three-quarters of all cases without the consent of the village meeting, often in the face of bitter opposition—of individual householders or small minority groups, can be credited as a success for the Stolypin policy only with reservations. It was only where entire village communities reached an amicable agreement to separate that the policy can be said to have achieved its real purpose. Such separations did indeed occur. Between 1 January 1906 and 1 January 1912, the surveyors of the land settlement organisation demarcated 520,000 farmsteads of individual separators (with 5,260,000 desyatins) and 370,000 farms (of 2,800,000 desyatins) resulting from collective separations. The farms already occupied by their owners or definitely offered to heads of households on 1 January 1913 numbered 74,000 (7,400,000 desyatins) for individual secessionists and 585,000 (4,360,000 desyatins) for "communal" ones. Less than half the secessions achieved, therefore, can be assumed to have taken place on a voluntary basis.

Communal separations moreover, were confined in the main to a few provinces. Thus during the first two years of the operation of land settlement, three-quarters of such separations were confined to six provinces. Clearly the consolidation of entire villages was a somewhat marginal process.

About the economic success of the new "Stolypin peasants"—and economic progress and prosperity had been the keynote of land settlement propaganda—the opinions of observers differed. These may reflect geographical differences; personal prejudices also may have played a part. Semyonov noted that separation led to economic advance but his farmstead, significantly, was located in the vicinity of Moscow. There separation facilitated the adoption of improved farming methods and machinery. Similarly in December 1913 prince Eugene Trubetskoy commented on the growth in the villages of prosperity, of a new social spirit and of a powerful petty bourgeoisie.

As against this Chernyshev, reviewing the effects of separation for the Free Economic Society, reported in 1911 that, at the time of his investigation

the abandonment of the land commune had not noticeably changed the character of cultivation either in case of those who remain communal holders or in the case of those who had left it.

Tyumenev, another observer, expressed the view that the transition to enclosed farming "did not justify the expectations of the authors of the Decree of November 9, 1906." These views lead Owen to the conclusion that

the technical development of *hutor* and *otrub* did not correspond with the advance in the assertion of rights of peasant private ownership. This weakness was due to land-shortage . . . and to peasant poverty. The degree to which enclosed farming was successful corresponds to the resources possessed by the more fortunate peasants.

This may be among the reasons why *khutors* in the northern half of the empire enjoyed a relative prosperity while those in the south did not.

Thus, whilst different statements show certain variations of emphasis, it is yet clear that, from a purely economic point of view, separation by itself did not prove the panacea for the low productivity of Russian agriculture. It did not create a "prosperous peasantry." While some of the better-off peasants—especially those already owning some private non-*nadel* land—flourished and became "landlord-peasants," many others remained smallholders continuing to live at subsistence level as they had done before. The economic success of the Stolypin reform was at best a partial one.

From the evidence which has been listed, certain conclusions emerge. From 1909 or 1910, well before the war of 1914 impeded their progress, land settlement operations were showing distinct signs of slowing down. They were confined, in the main, to the peripheral provinces of European Russia where the land commune had never gained a firm hold, where land was relatively abundant and where capitalist relationships were developing with comparative rapidity. Land settlement, on the other hand, had little impact on the central provinces where the peasant problem was most acute. Among the reasons for this was the fact that peasants, on the whole, opposed the new policy. Welcomed by a small minority, it was resisted by the rest, sometimes with great bitterness. The opposition, while not devoid of psychological and ideological elements was, in the main, based on material interests. Only a limited number of peasant households stood directly to gain from it. In many parts of the empire land settlement, for a variety of reasons, proved inappropriate. By a curious paradox, it appeared most relevant and practicable in precisely those parts of the empire where it was perhaps least needed from a social and political point of view. It may well be that, on an overall view, land settlement achieved little more than a "tidying up" by the elimination of the weakest marginal members of the peasantry. It also brought about some acceleration of the twin processes of consolidation and secession from the commune in regions where they were already under way. The available evidence, moreover, suggests that, contrary to expectation, its effect on peasant farming in the shape of improved methods and productivity was only marginal. The reform, in the majority of cases, could provide neither adequately sized holdings nor capital for serious improvement nor yet the level of education that would be needed to turn rural Russia into a second Denmark. In sum, the policy of land settlement at no time looked like providing an effective solution of Russia's peasant problem. Its actual contribution to such a solution was a modest one. It hardly required the object lesson of 1917 to show that, in all major respects, Stolypin's reform had proved a qualified failure. In many parts of Russia, as Witte had been at pains to warn the State Council, conditions were far from ripe for the introduction of individualist and capitalist farming methods.

It must, in the circumstances, appear more than doubtful whether the results achieved would have been significantly different if Stolypin's legislation had operated for twenty years instead of nine. Of course, during the additional years, there would have been some further progress in the direction desired. This, however, would probably have occurred largely as the result of spontaneous economic development: Stolypin's laws would have supplied little more than the legal and administrative framework. Peasant psychology, vested interests (many of them perfectly legitimate) and, above all, the economic "facts of life" (land shortage, unequal quality of land, shortage of capital) would have continued to impede the advance of land settlement. Kutler's estimate of a hundred years required for the success of the policy might well have proved nearer the mark than the twenty years stipulated by Stolypin.

Stolypin's land policy, in fact, need not have caused Lenin sleepless nights (or, for that matter, the social revolutionaries). There was never, as Wolfe suggests, a close race between Lenin and the ghost of the dead Stolypin. It was not land settlement which posed the major threat to Lenin's success. The most serious challenge in the villages came, on the contrary, from the followers of Chernov and Maria Spiridonova [Socialist Revolutionaries]. They— not land settlement—constituted in the realm of peasant affairs the competition which Lenin would have to beat.

The first burst of Russian industrialization came in the late 1880s and the 1890s, a period that has attracted much attention from economic historians of imperial Russia. A second major upswing occurred between 1905 and 1914, and it has received less emphasis. ALEXANDER GERSCHENKRON (b. 1904), Walter S. Baker Professor of Economics at Harvard University, has sought to put this latter period of economic growth in perspective in an essay covering the century after 1861, entitled "Patterns of Economic Development." In contrasting the 1890s and the post-1905 periods, he emphasizes the diminished reliance of industry on the policy of "substitutions," which the state had practiced earlier. For example, the state had substituted its own demand for iron and steel, for such projects as the Trans-Siberian Railroad, to make good the absence of a developed domestic market for these products. Gerschenkron is a distinguished economist and economic historian, the author of *Bread and Democracy in Germany, A Dollar Index of Soviet Machinery Output,* and *Economic Backwardness in Historical Perspective.**

Alexander Gerschenkron

Increasing Industrial Maturity

What happened in Russia in the nineties of the last century was the great upsurge of modern industrialization. Nevertheless, certain aspects of it were not modern at all. Several times before in the course of Russian history, economic development seemed to follow a curious pattern: the military interests of the state induced the government to bring about a rapid spurt of economic growth. In the course of the process, heavy burdens were imposed upon the peasant population of the country, the enserfment of the Russian peasantry having been inextricably connected with the policies of economic development. So great were the burdens, and so heavy the pressure, that after a number of years the spurt tended to peter out, leaving an exhausted population to recover slowly from the stress and the strain that had been imposed upon it.

There is little doubt that military considerations had a good deal to do with the Russian government's conversion to a policy of rapid industrialization. True, no immediate military discomfiture preceded

*Alexander Gerschenkron, "Patterns of Economic Development," reprinted by permission of the publishers from Cyril E. Black, editor, *The Transformation of Russian Society,* pp. 52–61. Cambridge, Mass.: Harvard University Press, Copyright, 1960, by the President and Fellows of Harvard College.

the initiation of the new policy. But the war of 1877 against the Turks was won on the battlefields in the Danube Valley and the Balkan Mountains, only to be lost in Berlin against the British and probably the Germans as well. In the course of the Berlin congress, particularly during its dramatic moments, the Russian government had much opportunity and reason to reflect that it was not much better prepared for any military conflict with a Western power than it had been a quarter of a century earlier on the eve of the Crimean War. In the short run, Russian reaction consisted in shifting the direction of its expansionist policy away from Europe to Central Asia and the Far East. Taking a somewhat longer view and further prompted by the formation of military alliances in Central Europe, the government turned toward the goal of a drastic increase in the economic potential of the country.

In the 1890's, a renewed enserfment of the peasantry was, of course, not in the realm of practical politics. Nor was there any need for such a measure. The reforms of rural administration which had been introduced with the advent of reaction under Alexander III gave the central bureaucracy sufficient tax-exacting power over the peasantry; at least for some time it was possible to keep the peasantry in the state of docile compliance. The joint responsibility of the village commune for tax payments was helpful, though far from indispensable. The considerable shift to indirect taxation further increased the government's ability to pay for the industrialization in conditions of a relative price and currency stability. The fiscal policy of the government was able to perform the function which at an earlier age had been performed by the institution of serfdom.

The great spurt of the 1890's came to an end in 1900. The depression of that year was variously interpreted as an overproduction crisis, a financial crash, or a response to economic setbacks abroad, particularly in Central Europe. It is fairly clear, however, that below the surface phenomena lay the exhaustion of the tax-paying powers of the rural population. The patience of the peasantry was at its end. The following years were characterized by growing unrest in the villages until the folly of the war with Japan fanned the isolated fires into the flame of a widespread peasant rebellion in the course of the 1905 Revolution. All this was very much like the consummation of the traditional pattern of Russian economic development: a quick upsurge compressed within a relatively short period ending in years of stagnation. And yet there was a great deal more to the industrial spurt of the 1890's than simply a repetition of previous sequences of economic development. It would seem more plausible to view those similarities as the last emanations, in prerevolutionary Russia, of the traditional pattern. For the differences were fully as important as the similarities. Also in this broad sense, the new and the old appeared curiously commingled. Along with the resurrection of a specifically Russian past, there was also the assimilation of Russian economic development into a graduated but still general pattern of European industrialization.

Two, and perhaps three, factors stand out in distinguishing the upswing of the 1890's from similar episodes in the more remote past. One of them has just been mentioned. During the decade of the 1890's, the Russian government abstained from introducing for the sake of the industrialization any far-reaching institutional change which, while aiding the process in the short run, would have become a serious obstacle to its continuation in the long run. Neither the institution of the *zemskii nachal'nik* [land captain] nor the additional steps taken in the 1890's to preserve and protect the village commune could of course compare in any way with the enserfment of the peasantry. That a government firmly committed to the policy of industrialization went out of its way to safeguard the obshchina [peasant commune] seemed paradoxical. But apart from the fiscal value of the arrangement, it was felt that its existence contributed to political stability within the country. Neither reason was persuasive. Satisfactory substitutes for joint responsibility for tax payments could easily have been found; and the events of the subsequent years showed clearly that the village commune nursed rebellious rather than conservative sentiments. The abolition of the commune still remained a problem of industrial policies in Russia, but it was one which antedated the period of rapid industrialization.

The other factor was positive. A modern industrialization based on the creation of fixed capital of considerable durability was not followed by periods of protracted stagnations as easily as had been the earlier, much more labor-intensive spurts of economic development ("stagnation" of course is to be understood simply in terms of a very low or even negative rate of growth). The recuperative power of a capital-intensive economy was greatly superior to that of its historical predecessors. And, finally, a modern industrialization is characterized also by a more substantial investment in human capital. In particular, it tends to bring about, over a relatively short period, a considerable change in entrepreneurial and managerial attitudes as well as, though to a lesser extent, in those of skilled labor. All this means that the effects of the great spurt reached out strongly into the future; that the process of industrialization could be resumed at diminished *faux frais* and in a form more efficient and less dependent upon the support of the state.

Such were the characteristic features of Russian industrial growth in the years between the 1905 Revolution and the outbreak of World War I. This, too, was a period of rather rapid growth (some 6 per cent per year), even though the rate of change remained below that of the 1890's. During those years industrialization could no longer be the primary concern of the government. War and revolution had greatly strained budgetary capabilities. The redemption payments (as well as the institution of joint responsibility) had disappeared under the impact of the revolution. Kokovtsev, first as Minister of Finance and later as head of the Cabinet, pursued a cautious policy of thrift. Railroad building continued, but on a much reduced scale. The execution of such armament plans as were conceived was being postponed from year to year. In the eighteenth century, the death of Peter the Great and the withdrawal of the state from active economic policy spelled the doom of the contemporaneous economic development. But in Russia of the twentieth century, Count Witte's fall and the abandonment of his policies did not prevent a renewed outburst of industrial activity.

Nothing underscores more clearly the changed attitude of the government than the fact that its most important action in the field of economic policy was Stolypin's legislation against the obshchina. In a radical reversal of the agrarian policies pursued only a few years earlier, Stolypin's reforms of 1906 and 1910 made it possible for the peasants to sever their connection with the obshchina through a simple and advantageous procedure, to acquire personal ownership of the land, and in the process often to swap the numerous strips of their former allotment for a single consolidated holding.

There is no question that many aspects of the reform were harsh and unfair to the less prosperous members of the village communes. There is also every evidence that the government's *volte-face* was caused by political considerations, that is to say, by the impressive lesson learned from peasant uprisings during the preceding revolution. The consequences of the reform for the process of industrial development were accidental from the government's point of view, despite some liberal phraseology ("liberal" in the European sense of the term) used in defending the reforms.

Nevertheless, the potential positive effects of the reform on industrial development were indisputable. The authors of the reform, despite considerable opposition within the government, refused to accept the concept of family or household ownership; the ownership of peasants leaving the village commune was vested in the head of the household. For the first time, the road was open for an unimpaired movement to the city of peasant family members; for the first time large groups of Russian peasants could, like their counterparts in the West sell the land and use the proceeds for establishing themselves outside agriculture. The war of 1914 necessarily cut short the implementation of the reform, but its initial effect was considerable. Both those peasants who had felt that leaving the commune would enable them to increase the productivity of their farms and those peasants who had been anxious to leave the village hastened to avail themselves of the separation procedure. It was a considerable step on the road of Russia's westernization.

And this is the aspect of the reform that is of primary importance from the point of view of the present discussion. The economic stagnation that followed the reign of Peter the Great was burdened by the legacy of serfdom. The very modernization of the state machinery under Peter meant that the government was much better equipped to enforce the serfdom condition upon the peasantry and to deal effectively with fugitives from serf status. At the same time, the territorial expansion of Russia kept reducing and making more remote the frontier regions which formerly had been the sanctuary of so many peasants in their flight from oppression. It was under these conditions that the edict granting the nobility and the gentry freedom from service obligations marked the acme of the state's retirement from active guidance of the country's economic life. That act finally severed the original connection between serfdom and economic development and sealed the perpetuation of serfdom as a main obstacle to economic progress. With regard to both its historical locus and its "liberalizing" character, the Imperial Edict of Peter III (1762) bears a certain resemblance to Stolypin's reform. And yet, despite these similarities, it is the difference between the two measures which may be taken as a gauge of the contrast in historical situations. The great spurt under Peter the Great had not led to sustained growth. The traditional pattern of Russian economic development was allowed to work itself out fully. By contrast, the withdrawal of the state after the upswing of the 1890's was marked by a measure which was designed to further rather than thwart industrial progress.

The westernization of Russian industrialization between 1906 and 1914 expressed itself in a large variety of ways. To use the previously adopted terminology, one could say that the pattern of substitutions was changing rapidly. To some extent banks stepped into the vacuum left by the state. In this way, credit-creation policies and some entrepreneurial guidance by the banks continued to substitute for the scarcity of both capital and entrepreneurship in Russia. But this mode of substitution tended to approximate the pattern of Russian development to that prevailing in Central Europe. The credit policies of the banks were still a substitute for an autonomous internal market, but there is little doubt that one of the consequences of the industrial creations of the nineties was the gradual emergence of such a market.

It may be quite tempting to view again the change between the period under review and that of the 1890's in terms of Erik Dahmén's dichotomy between development blocks in the state of full completion and development blocks in the beginning stage. The years 1906–1914 were characterized by the relative scarcities of coal, oil, and metals, in conjunction with the rapid forging ahead of metal-processing industries. There is a persistent and very much exaggerated tendency in present Russian historiography to present those scarcities as consequences of monopolistic policies in the basic-materials industries. It is probably more reasonable, still following Dahmén, to say that during the years preceding the First World War the structure of Russian industry was distinguished by specific disproportionalities and that once again, though on a much higher level, industry may have been passing through a period of dynamic preparation for another great spurt. Such a spurt, of course, never materialized. The point, however, is that considering the years 1906–1914 as a period of formation of new development blocks may help to explain why the rate of growth during those years was not higher than it was. It cannot explain the high growth that was actually attained in a situation where the outside aid to industry had manifestly declined to a fraction of its previous volume. It is more helpful, therefore, to regard this period as governed by the effects of diminished backwardness, and in this sense to view the whole stretch between the end of the 1880's and the outbreak of the war as consisting of two

disparate and yet connected parts: the great spurt of the 1890's had prepared for the subsequent continuation of growth under changed conditions.

Many of the tensions and frictions that could be so strikingly observed during the 1890's reappeared in the second period, if at all, in a considerably modified and tempered form. There is no question that great progress had taken place with regard to entrepreneurial attitudes. Without such progress and, in particular, without the general rise in trustworthiness of Russian businessmen, the banks could never have come to play a powerful role as suppliers of long-term credit to industrial firms. The general modernization of entrepreneurial attitudes no doubt made the complex of actions and relations of the individual entrepreneurs less heterogeneous. The decline in the importance of the government as an economic agent pointed in the same direction.

The years that had passed since the second half of the 1880's considerably increased the stock of permanent industrial labor in the country. At the same time, after 1905, more tangible improvements both in real wages and in working conditions became noticeable. The reduction in the importance of foreign engineers and foremen in factories and mines also tended to diminish friction. At the same time, the great pressure upon the peasantry had subsided. In contrast to the last decades of the nineteenth century, the quantity of breadgrain available for domestic consumption rose faster than did the population. The industrialization between 1906 and 1914 no longer offers a picture of a race against time and of progressive exhaustion, physically and mentally, of the population's power to suffer and to endure.

Those elements of relaxation and "normalization" in the industrial process should not, however, disguise the fact that in other respects the great spurt of the 1890's, the industrial upsurge under conditions of extreme backwardness, still dominated the course of the development in the later period. The composition of the growing industry continued to favor the same branches as before. As in the earlier period, the stress on bigness was characteristic of both the productive and the organizational structure. The movement toward cartelization, which was mentioned before, must be regarded as a part of this continued emphasis on bigness. As was true in countries west of Russia, the policies of the banks tended to accelerate the process. In this sense they were the true heirs to the policies previously pursued by the bureaucracy. And like the latter, they tended to exaggerate and accelerate the process both for good and bad reasons. Interest in small enterprises would have strained the organizational and supervisory powers of the banks as it had proved unmanageable for the bureaucracy. On the other hand, just as many a civil servant had found opportunities for personal enrichment in his official connection with large enterprises, similarly increases in capital, mergers, and mediation of monopolistic agreements, also when not required by the process of growth, proved a considerable source of profit for the banks. Still, when everything is said and done, it was of utmost importance that the stress on large-scale business, the very essence of industrialization in conditions of backwardness and the basis for its successful implementation, could be preserved after the withdrawal of the state.

Russia before the First World War was still a relatively backward country by any quantitative criterion. The large weight of the agrarian sector of the economy and the low level of the national per capita output placed her far below and behind neighboring Germany. Nevertheless, as far as the general pattern of its industrialization in the second period was concerned, Russia seemed to duplicate what had happened in Germany in the last decades of the nineteenth century. One might surmise that in the absence of the war Russia would have continued on the road of progressive westernization.

It is not entirely pointless to speculate on what might have happened in the course of such a development. Diminution of backwardness is a complex process. As has already been noted, certain paraphernalia of backwardness are shed fairly soon after the beginning of the process. Other elements are more resistant to change. Thus, the great school of industrialization tends to educate the entrepreneurs before it educates the workers; and it takes still longer before the influence of the industrial sector of the economy penetrates into the countryside and begins to affect the attitudes of the peasantry. In the latter respect, prerevolutionary Russia saw no more than the first modest traces of such an influence. Yet the likelihood that the transformation in agriculture would have gone on at an accelerated speed is very great.

In addition to the age-long attitudes which are more or less rapidly modified under the impact of economic development, there are specific institutional and economic factors which are created in the very process of industrialization, and which often appear strange and incomprehensible from the point of view of an advanced country. But they are the stuff that industrialization in backward areas is made of. Some of them disappear after they have fulfilled their mission, teleologically speaking. Thus did the Russian government leave the economic scene after the upswing of the 1890's. It is again extremely likely that the banks would not have been able to keep their ascendancy over Russian industry for a very long time to come. Diminishing scarcity of capital, further improvements in the quality of entrepreneurship, and the sheer growth of industrial enterprises in all probability would have in due time enhanced the position of industrial firms to a point where they no longer needed the banks' guidance. That is what happened in Germany after 1900, and the natural course of events might well have moved Russian industry in the same direction. Even so, if the German example had predictive value, the banks would not have necessarily been transformed into the English type of commercial bank. They would have retained their interest in long-term investments, and in this sense the Russian economy would have remained characterized by a peculiarity created in the earlier stages of its development. Even more important, the stress on bigness, the specific composition of industrial output, and the significance of cartels and trusts within the industrial structure are likely to have increased rather than diminished over the years. One of the curious aspects of the European development was that the process of assimilation of backward countries to advanced countries was by no means a one-sided affair. To some extent, as the degree of backwardness was reduced, the backward country tended to become more like the advanced country. Yet precisely because in the process of its industrialization the backward country had been forced to make use of very modern technological and economic instruments, in the long run it was the advanced country that in some respects assimilated its economy to that of the backward country. A comparison of the structure of, say, the German and the English economy in 1900 and some decades later would serve to illustrate this point.

Russian industrial development around the turn of the century was frequently decried as "artificial." Count Witte used to reject the accusation with considerable vehemence as meaningless and irrelevant (probably with justice). For what matters is both the degree and the direction of "artificiality" or "spontaneity" in the process seen over an appropriately long time. Taking into consideration the economic conditions that prevailed in Russia prior to its great spurt of industrialization, it is difficult to deny that the Russian development fitted well into the general pattern of European industrialization, conceived, as it properly should be, in terms of a graduated rather than a uniform pattern.

The only purpose in speculating about the probable course of Russian economic development as it might have been, if not interrupted by war and revolution, is to try to cast more light on the general industrial trends that dominated the last period of industrialization in prerevolutionary Russia. Still the question remains whether war and revolution cannot be interpreted as the result of the preceding industrial development. Some Soviet historians certainly incline in that direction. If the Russian bourgeoisie could be saddled with the main responsibility for the outbreak of the war and if, in addition, it could be shown that in bringing about the war it had acted in response to the pressure of its economic interests—if, in short, the process of Russian industrialization carried in itself the seeds of the coming military conflict—then to abstract the war from the process in order to elucidate the course and prospects of Russian industrialization would mean to abstract the process as well. Some Russian manufacturers indeed may have welcomed the wartime orders for their products. Yet the precise mechanism through which such interests of the bourgeoisie were in fact translated into the decisions reached by the emperor and his government has remained altogether obscure.

The view just described seems to magnify the political significance of the Russian bourgeoisie out of all proportion and to substitute suppositions of various degrees of plausibility for historical evidence. It might be more persuasive to argue that the government saw a relatively short and victorious war as a chance to solidify the regime and to avert the danger of revolution. And the question then would be to what extent the preceding industrial development may be said to have been leading to another revolutionary cataclysm.

It is true, of course, that the social and political structure of the empire was shot through with manifold serious weaknesses. Opposition to the regime was nearly universal among the intelligentsia and certainly widespread among the industrial and mercantile groups. Since 1912, the year of the famous massacre in the Lena gold fields, the strike movement of the workers was again gaining momentum. And at the bottom of the social edifice there was the old resentment of the peasants who had never accepted the rightfulness of the gentry's ownership rights over the land. The peasantry's land hunger was a steady source of ferment. The sentiment in the villages was no doubt further exacerbated by the blows struck against the village commune and the threat of its dissolution. A new outbreak of revolutionary violence at some point was far from being altogether improbable.

And yet, as one compares the situation in the years before 1914 with that of the nineties, striking differences are obvious. In the earlier period, the very process of industrialization with its powerful confiscatory pressures upon the peasantry kept adding, year in and year out, to the feelings of resentment and discontent until the outbreak of large-scale disorders became almost inevitable. The industrial prosperity of the following period had no comparable effects, however. Modest as the improvements in the situation of peasants were, they were undeniable and widely diffused. Those improvements followed rather than preceded a revolution and accordingly tended to contribute to a relaxation of tension. Stolypin's reforms certainly were an irritant, but after the initial upsurge their implementation was bound to proceed in a much more gradual fashion.

Similarly, the economic position of labor was clearly improving. In the resurgence of the strike movement economic problems seemed to predominate. It is true, of course, that in the specific conditions of the period any wage conflict tended to assume a political character because of the ready interventions of police and military forces on behalf of management. But this did not mean that the climate of opinion and emotion within the labor movement was becoming more revolutionary; as shown by the history of European countries (such as Austria or Belgium), sharp political struggles marked the period of formation of labor movements that in actual fact, though not always in the language used, were committed to reformism. There is little doubt that the Russian labor movement of those years was slowly turning toward revision and trade-unionist lines. As was true in the West, the struggles for general and equal franchise to the Duma and for a cabinet responsible to the Duma, which probably would have occurred sooner or later, may well have further accentuated this development. To repeat, I do not mean to deny that there was much political instability in the country. There clearly was. What matters here is that from the point of view of the industrial development of the country, war, revolution, or the threat thereof may reasonably be seen as extraneous phenomena. In this sense, it seems plausible to say that Russia on the eve of the war was well on the way toward a westernization or, perhaps more precisely, a Germanization of its industrial growth. The "old" in the Russian economic system was definitely giving way to the "new." It was left to the regime that finally emerged from the 1917 Revolution, generated in the misery of the war and the shame of defeats, to create a different set of novelties and to mix them with old ingredients of Russian economic history in the strange and powerful infusion of Soviet industrialism.

The official textbook on the history of the Communist party of the Soviet Union occupies a special place in Russian historiography. Since Stalin introduced his "Short Course" on this subject in 1938 (replaced in 1959 by a de-Stalinized version), this has been the most widely read kind of history book in the Soviet Union, a virtual gospel for party indoctrination. It was prepared by historians of the Institute of Marxism-Leninism of the Central Committee of the Communist party of the Soviet Union, under the direction of a senior ideologist, BORIS N. PONOMAREV (b. 1905). While the academic Soviet historians and the official party historians concur in discerning a revolutionary situation in Russia in 1914, the party historians place special emphasis on the position of the Bolsheviks and their rivals. The dogmatic, moralistic tone of passages dealing with the "Victory" of the Bolsheviks over the Mensheviks calls for skepticism. On the other hand, confidential communications among the tsarist police *and* among the Mensheviks in this period led to some of the same conclusions about the strength of the two main factions in Russian Marxism at this time. The statistical data that are used to rebut interpretations such as Gerschenkron's are on the whole reliable, which is not to say that they necessarily prove the existence of a revolutionary situation.*

Boris N. Ponomarev

The Approaching Revolutionary Crisis

A new economic and political situation arose in Russia in 1910–1911. Beginning with 1910, industrial stagnation was succeeded by a boom. Coal output rose from nearly 26 million tons in 1909 to nearly 36 million in 1913, pig-iron from under 3 million tons to over 4½ million, steel from just over 3 million tons to nearly 5 million, with increases in the output of textiles and sugar.

The post-revolutionary years [post-1905] saw the rapid development of imperialism in Russia. There was a marked increase in the concentration of production and capital, with monopoly concerns dominating nearly every branch of industry and transport. In iron, for instance, the Prodamet syndicate controlled more than 80 per cent of total output, and in coal another syndicate, Produgol, controlled

---

*From Boris N. Ponomarev (ed.), *History of the Communist Party of the Soviet Union* (Moscow: Foreign Languages Publishing House, 1960). pp. 162–165, 168–169, 175–176, 181–183. Anonymously translated from the Russian edition of 1960.

three-quarters of the Donets coalfield output. Over 80 per cent of the assets of the joint-stock banks were concentrated in 12 big banks. The financial oligarchy was steadily extending its domination over the country's economic life and merging more closely with the bureaucratic upper levels of the government machine.

There was a greater inflow of foreign capital. By 1914, approximately one-third of all industrial shares, and over two-fifths of the capital of the principal banks, were held by the West European bourgeoisie. Foreign capitalists held sway in such key industries as coal, oil and metalworking, and their annual profits from investments and loans ran into hundreds of millions of rubles. Tsarist Russia was becoming more and more dependent upon West European imperialism.

A handful of European and Russian capitalist magnates were growing richer, while the people were growing poorer. The landlords, capitalists and kulaks appropriated about three-quarters of the national income. Hundreds of thousands of people were forced to emigrate in search of work. Over one and a half million left the country in the first ten years of the century.

The cost of living was rising, and the position of the worker was deteriorating. An official industrial survey revealed that while annual wages averaged 246 rubles, annual profit per worker averaged 252 rubles. The greater part of the working day was thus passed in work for the capitalist. The workers' life and health were cheap in tsarist Russia. The "Accident Compensation Table" at the big Obukhov shipbuilding and engineering works in St. Petersburg allowed 100 rubles' compensation for complete blindness, 35 rubles for loss of one eye, 50 rubles for total loss of hearing, and 40 rubles for loss of speech.

Incredible poverty reigned in the countryside. Stolypin's agrarian policy had, as its direct result, the mass impoverishment of the peasants and enrichment of the kulak blood-suckers. The number of farms with one horse or no horse at all increased by nearly two million between the turn of the century and 1912. The Russian countryside presented a picture of omnipotent feudal landlords, bigger and richer kulak farms, the impoverishment of a vast mass of middle peasants, and a substantially increased mass of landless peasants or rural proletarians. The tsarist government had attempted to remove some of these contradictions by settling several million peasants from European Russia in Siberia; but this policy failed completely. The peasants would sell all their property and move to Siberia, only to return penniless and rebellious.

Contradictions within the rural community became sharper. The peasant's chief enemy was still the feudal landlord. But there was also sharper conflict between the kulak and the poor peasant. Cases of peasants setting fire to manor houses and kulak farmsteads became more frequent after 1910. On top of this came the terrible famine of 1911, which affected some 30 million peasants. The situation left no doubt whatever that the Stolypin policy had collapsed.

Its collapse brought out more saliently than ever the profound contradictions throughout Russia's social and political system. It demonstrated anew that the tsarist government was incapable of solving the country's basic social and economic problems.

The remnants of serfdom were an intolerable obstacle to national development. Though Russia had taken the capitalist path, every year that passed saw her lagging further and further behind the advanced capitalist countries. Lenin wrote in 1913 that, though in the half century since the emancipation of the peasants iron consumption had increased fivefold, Russia still remained a backward country, equipped with modern machinery four times worse than Britain, five times worse than Germany and ten times worse than the United States. In 1900 Russia led the world in oil production; some ten years later she was behind other countries. Poverty, oppression, lack of human rights, humiliating indignities imposed on the people—all this, Lenin emphasised, was in crying contradiction to the state of the country's productive forces and to the degree of political understanding and demands of the masses, awakened by the first Russian revolution. Only a new revolution could save Russia.

No amount of savage Stolypin repression could eradicate the people's urge for freedom and a better life. The fatigue of the masses was passing; hatred of the oppressors was coming to the surface with ever greater force.

The working class was the first to take the offensive. The years of revolution and reaction had taught the workers much and had raised their class consciousness. They had grown considerably in numbers since the beginning of the century. In 1913, there were already about 3,500,000 workers in industry alone, and they were more highly concentrated than in any other country. Over half (53.4 per cent) worked in factories employing 500 workers or more, whereas in the United States the proportion was about one-third.

In the summer of 1910 strikes broke out in Moscow. They gave an impetus to the movement, and towards the end of the year there were political demonstrations in St. Petersburg, Moscow and other towns, followed by student rallies and strikes. The movement continued to mount throughout 1911, with over 105,000 workers, or double the number as compared with the preceding year, involved in strike stoppages. The year ended with powerful demonstrations at St. Petersburg factories in support of the

Social-Democrats' Duma interpellation on the frame-up trial of the Social-Democrat members of the Second Duma. The Bolshevik demand for their release was supported by the workers.

The Bolsheviks' prediction that a new revolutionary upsurge was inevitable proved to be true. Everywhere there was growing discontent and indignation among the people. The workers saw in the Bolshevik revolutionary slogans a clear-cut expression of their own aspirations. An important part in bringing these slogans home to the masses was played by the Bolshevik weekly legal newspaper, *Zvezda (Star)*, which began publication in St. Petersburg towards the end of 1910.

The opportunists played a particularly harmful and ignominious role in this new revolutionary revival. Instead of revolutionary struggle, the liquidators and Trotskyists called for a "petition campaign," urging the workers to sign a petition to the Duma requesting "freedom of coalition" (freedom of association, assembly, strikes, etc.). The Bolsheviks explained to the workers that there could be no freedom as long as the country remained in the hands of the Black-Hundred landlords. Freedom for the people could be won only with the overthrow of the monarchy. The clamorous "petition campaign" proved a fiasco: the liquidators collected barely 1,300 signatures, whereas the Bolshevik slogans had the solid support of hundreds of thousands of workers.

These strikes, political demonstrations and rallies, together with the peasant actions against the landlords and kulaks, were the harbingers of a new revolution. Could the proletariat perform its role as leader in this maturing revolutionary struggle of the mass of the people? That depended, to a decisive extent, on the state of the Marxist party of the Russian working class.

The new revolutionary struggles posed the urgent need to strengthen the Party and formulate the new tasks in leading the mass revolutionary movement.

The formal uniting of Bolsheviks and Mensheviks within a single R.S.D.L.P. [Russian Social Democratic Labor party] during the revolution had led to a peculiar situation and had predetermined what the Bolsheviks had to do within the Party. The Bolsheviks had set themselves the task of cleansing the Party of opportunist elements through ideological struggle. They had accomplished much in that respect. Nearly all the illegal Party organisations were Bolshevik. The Menshevik betrayal of the proletariat had gone so far that the Party membership was coming to realise more and more the need for a complete break with the liquidators and their expulsion from the Party.

The Bolsheviks began to prepare energetically for a Party conference. The liquidators, Trotskyists and conciliators made frenzied but futile attempts to prevent a conference taking place, and thereby block the consolidation of the Party on Bolshevik principles. In the summer of 1911, G. K. Orzhonikidze, I. I. Schwarz (Semyon) and other Party workers were sent to Russia. At a conference of leading Party committees, a Russian Organisation Commission (R.O.C.) was set up. It carried out a vast amount of organising and propaganda work in preparation for the conference.

The Sixth All-Russian Conference of the R.S.D.L.P. was held in Prague on January 5–17, 1912, and was attended by delegates from more than twenty Party organisations. . . .

The Prague Conference played an outstanding part in building the Bolshevik Party, a party of a new type. It *summed up* a whole historical period of Bolshevik struggle against Menshevism, and *consolidated the victory* of the Bolsheviks, retaining the banner of the Russian Social-Democratic Labor Party firmly in their hands. Factionalism was thus eliminated within the Party and its leadership, the Central Committee, and this was of exceptional importance for the Party's continued growth and for enhancing its role in the revolutionary struggle. . . .

The workers' movement continued to grow in scope and strength. There were over one million strikers in 1912, and 1,272,000 in 1913. Economic struggles were intertwined with political ones, and culminated in mass revolutionary strikes. The working class went over to the offensive against the capitalists and the tsarist monarchy. . . .

The strikes were of national importance: they aroused wide masses of the people and spurred them on to action. In 1910–1914, according to patently minimised figures, there were over 13,000 peasant outbreaks, in which many manor houses and kulak farmsteads were destroyed, and grain, cattle and farm equipment confiscated. The unrest spread to the tsarist army. In July, 1912, a sapper unit stationed in Turkestan mutinied; in January, 1913, there was unrest in the Kiev garrison; mutiny was brewing in the Baltic and Black Sea fleets.

A new revolution was maturing in Russia. . . .

Together with the rise of the working-class movement, the party of the working class, the Bolshevik Party, grew and gained in strength. After the hard years of reaction, and amidst the difficulties created by their illegal status, the Bolsheviks *re-established a mass party,* firmly led and guided by its Central Committee and the latter's Russian and Foreign Bureau. The Party published a widely-read daily newspaper, had a parliamentary group, several regional, and a number of city committees, nuclei in many factories and mills, and

Party groups in workers' legal organisations. The Central Committee maintained contact with nearly 100 organisations and groups throughout the country, from Vladivostok to Warsaw and from Vologda to Tashkent. The Central Committee and local organisations reacted with leaflets to every major development in the life of the country. Despite continuous police persecution, the Party was able to publish in addition to *Pravda*, the legal magazines *Prosveshcheniye (Enlightenment), Voprosy Strakhovaniya (Social Insurance), Rabotnitsa (Woman Worker)* and conduct a number of trade union journals in a Bolshevik spirit.

The Party led every form of proletarian struggle. It organised the fight for the "partial demands" of the workers, integrating the economic needs and political interests of the proletariat. It taught the workers to react to every major manifestation and every crime of tsarist tyranny.

Of special importance for the revolutionary and class education of the proletariat were the annual illegal May Day meetings and the commemoration of Bloody Sunday, and the Lena shootings. In recalling these memorable stages of the struggle, the Party conducted its campaign beforehand, calling on the workers to strike and demonstrate on these days. The police, for all its skill in repression, was powerless to prevent the workers responding to the Bolshevik appeals. On January 22, 1913, about 200,000 workers went on strike, and the following year the number was 250,000. The May Day gatherings in 1913 were attended by 420,000 workers, and by more than half a million in 1914.

Everywhere—in mass strikes, street demonstrations, factory gate meetings— the Bolsheviks emphasised that revolution was the only way out, and put forward slogans expressing the people's longings; a democratic republic, an 8-hour working day, confiscation of the landed estates in favour of the peasants. News of these revolutionary strikes and revolutionary demands of the workers reached peasant huts and army barracks. In the revolutionary struggle of the workers the peasants, driven to despair by the exploitation of the landlords, and the soldiers, furious at the tyrannous conditions to which they were subjected, saw an example for themselves to follow.

The working class thus became the leader of the revolution, its standard-bearer, training and organising the masses for victory.

Meanwhile the waves of the working-class movement rose higher and higher. In the first half of 1914 about 1,500,000 workers were involved in strikes. One strike followed another. The strikes on the anniversary of Bloody Sunday were followed by stoppages in protest against the mass poisoning of women workers at a number of St. Petersburg factories. After May Day came the general strike in Baku, a courageous struggle supported by the workers of St. Petersburg, Moscow and other cities. On July 3 the police opened fire on a workers' meeting at the Putilov Works in St. Petersburg. A wave of indignation swept over the country. The St. Petersburg Bolshevik Committee called for immediate strike action. On July 4, 90,000 workers downed tools, on the 7th, 130,000, and on the 11th, 200,000. Demonstrations began in protest against the actions of the tsarist authorities and the war, which everyone felt was about to break out. The strike wave spread to Moscow; barricades were thrown up in St. Petersburg, Baku and Lodz.

Russia was faced with a revolutionary crisis. The landlords and capitalists were accusing each other of inability to put out the flames of revolution. One Black-Hundred newspaper came out with the eloquent headline: "Badaev to the Gallows!" [He was a Bolshevik Duma deputy.]

and called for the physical extermination of the working-class leaders. The tsarist government adopted "emergency" measures, the capital was turned into a veritable military camp. *Pravda* was closed down on June 25; wholesale arrests of Bolsheviks began.

The advance of the revolution was interrupted by the outbreak of the world war.

How would Lenin have appraised the chances for a revolutionary overthrow of the tsarist government on the eve of World War I? Despite his optimism during the Revolution of 1905–1907, the future founder of the Soviet state was not in fact at all optimistic about his prospects for success in the near future, perhaps in his own lifetime. Indeed, the student of the travails of Bolshevism in 1907–1914 is likely to agree that Lenin's doubts were only prudent. In emigration and in the underground, factional strife and police repression certainly seemed to curtail the impact of the professional revolutionaries. For all their slender numbers and harried condition, the prewar Bolsheviks have been the object of intensive historical study, both by Soviet and non-Soviet historians. A specialist in this area is HAROLD SHUKMAN (b. 1931), lecturer in modern Russian history at Oxford University and fellow of St. Antony's College there. In addition to writing *Lenin and the Russian Revolution* he has translated various Russian literary works and is presently preparing a major history of the Bolshevik movement in collaboration with L. S. Schapiro.*

Harold Shukman

Difficulties Among the Revolutionaries

The Stolypin period was for the Social Democrats the time of their greatest estrangement from Russia and Russian affairs, of their minimum impact on the workers. As a result, the party itself became once again the object and main concern of its leaders. Every possible issue became the excuse for a new sub-division in one or another faction. Lenin's own apparatus, such as it was in those lean years, was divided at its head, the Bolshevik Centre, over the faction's Duma policy, and over Lenin's drive for a final and total break with the Mensheviks. In four years, from 1903 to 1907, Lenin had used the device of a party congress four times to establish his position and solidify his support. Now it would be ten years before the next party congress was convened to define the Bolshevik identity, and then, ironically, Lenin would be absent.

The unity of the party was threatened not only by Lenin's divisive and monopolistic attitudes. The Mensheviks were outraged by his continued use of the "expropriations" as a means of financing his factional operations. Apart from the "expropriations," the Bolsheviks ran a succession of dubious financial operations, in secret from the Menshevik and other members of the Central Committee, which eventually became notorious. For instance, Lenin despatched two of his own agents to extort an inheritance from two sisters called Schmidt, whose father had left his estate to the entire party. Both agents married the girls to secure the funds, but the first one had to be threatened with his life before he could be made to part with his share, amounting to 100,000 roubles, or £10,000. The second, who became better known later as the Comintern agent, Victor Taratuta, succeeded in transferring into the Bolshevik coffers a sum of around £28,000. Again, the Bolsheviks diverted funds intended for the whole party from the estate of Morozov, the Moscow millionaire. As much as ideology, the continual jealous struggle for control of the party's funds, especially in view of the prodigious sums involved, made unity impossible.

Lenin's espousal of shady methods, and shadier operators to apply them, also alarmed some Bolsheviks. But his explanation was tough and realistic: "This isn't a school for young ladies. . . . Sometimes a crook is useful to us just because he is a crook." When Lenin proposed Taratuta as a Central Committee candidate he justified him as "an intelligent crook." Taratuta would stoop lower than anyone else in order to serve the Party's interests, and therefore he was of particular value in Lenin's eyes. Lenin's negligence of party honour led many of his closest associates to desert him. His compromise over the Duma, his devious attitude towards the Mensheviks—working for a split but keeping up the pretence of unity—and his continued resort to criminal methods, all

combined to brand him an opportunist in the eyes of some of his old comrades, not least those who like Bogdanov and Krasin had been his enthusiastic executives in precisely these operations: such firebrands would brook no compromise.

Life in exile, particularly the renewed, second spell, after the failure of 1905, was a moral and emotional ordeal. In a letter to Gorky, Lenin wrote in 1910 that exile was a hundred times harder than before 1905, and that exile and squabbles were inseparable. It was harder to keep up the monolithic front of revolutionary zeal and camaraderie in the aftermath of 1905, not that the latter had ever been easy for the Russian Social Democrats. . . .

The fractiousness and jealous truculence of Russian Social Democrats on the eve of the war was cogently expressed by Rosa Luxemburg. Writing to Kautsky about a plan to call a conference of all the rival Russian groups, in an effort once and for all to settle their fight over the party's funds, she said that it was a foolish idea, for such a conference would only be attended by a "handful of fighting cocks *living abroad . . . and to expect anything of these* cocks is pure delusion. They are already so . . . embittered, that a general confab will merely give them an opportunity to unburden themselves of their old, oldest and freshest insults. . . ."

The issues between the factions, and between Lenin and his own Bolshevik dissidents, assumed as always their own labels, convenient as targets of abuse and factional crusades. Thus Bolsheviks who resisted Lenin's splitting tactics and worked for party unity were dubbed "Conciliators," a word which was common party usage to describe the Kadets' and Octobrists' supposed relations with the government. On the other hand, the left-wing Bolsheviks, under Bogdanov's influence, who attacked the Social Democrat deputies in the Duma for their caution and campaigned to have them "recalled," received the title of "recallists" and their deviation "Recallism."

Some Mensheviks Lenin found guilty of a particularly heinous heresy: realising that the party apparatus was in ruins and under permanent threat from the police, these Mensheviks called on the party to concentrate its efforts on whatever legal activities could serve the workers' cause, such as trade unions, cooperatives, and supporting progressive legislation in the Duma. This approach was bad enough, and earned for them the Leninist curse of Reformism. But they went further and averred that these legal activities of the party should no longer be controlled by the underground centre, but should be left to develop organically in the prevailing social conditions.

To Lenin this was mutiny against central authority. To make his case stronger he, as always, overstated it and claimed that the movement was in favour of *liquidating* the party apparatus, though this was not intended. "Liquidationism" was perhaps the most serious hindrance to unity, assuming that unity had any chance whatever, for it also split the Mensheviks. In 1909 Plekhanov rallied those Mensheviks who stood for "the party," meaning the underground apparatus, and this group gained the title of "partyists."

During these years Russian Social Democracy was hopelessly divided and in perpetual conflict. Parallel conferences of factions took place repeatedly, each claiming to represent true opinion. Yet there still existed a continuing movement towards reconciliation and unification. It expressed the Social Democratic element in the Russian revolutionary tradition: the desire to create and develop a mass party. Though this goal was remote indeed, attempts were made to present a more coherent leadership as a prerequisite for success among the masses.

An All-Russian Conference which took place in Paris in January 1909 mustered a mere sixteen voting delegates: five Bolsheviks, three Mensheviks, five Polish Social Democrats, and three *Bundists*. Lenin used this occasion to secure a formal condemnation of both the Bolshevik "recallists" and the Menshevik "liquidators."

In January 1910 all the factions and groups of the party met in Paris for a conference of the Central Committee. Fourteen voting delegates attended, including Bolsheviks, Mensheviks, Polish Social Democrats, Letts, the *Bund,* and a dissident Bolshevik group called *Vperedists,* after the newspaper they published *(Forward)*. In addition, there were non-voting representatives of the party Central Organ *Sotsial-Demokrat* (Lenin); the Bolshevik factional paper *Proletarii* (Kamenev); the Menshevik factional paper *Golos Sotsial-Demokrata* (Martov); and finally Trotsky, who was most active in attempting to unite the party by means of the voluntary disbanding of all factions, and who represented his own small non-factional group, which published its paper, *Pravda,* in Vienna.

In an apparent spirit of reconciliation the January meetings of the Central Committee achieved an illusory agreement to disband the factions and discontinue rival publications. A united editorial board, consisting of Lenin, Zinoviev, Martov, Dan and a Polish representative, was to publish the party organ *Sotsial-Demokrat.* The assembly also adopted a number of decisions which were meant to resolve doctrinal and tactical differences between the various factions and splinter groups. Thus it castigated all forms of extremism in the party, including the left-wing "recallists" and the right-wing "liquidators." In an attempt to unite "all and sundry," the Mensheviks succeeded in getting approval for an invitation to the "liquidators" to take part in the illegal Central Committee in Russia. At the same time the conference recognised the legitimacy of Trotsky's group as well as the Bolshevik *Vpered* group, and they were encouraged to continue their activities as components of the party as a whole.

But no amount of conciliatory feeling could hide the fact that, whatever bodies and offices the party set up in apparent unity, it was invariably on a factional basis that they were compelled to appoint members. The pattern of the Central Committee itself was applied to all party organs, a plain recognition that factional interests would continue.

Lenin's attitude to the new climate was unmistakably contemptuous. Unity had always had a special connotation for him when it was the slogan and creation of others: it meant the good-humoured, flabby lack of resolve and "trading in principles" that a sinking of past differences implied, and it presaged doom. Unification of "all and sundry" meant to him the contamination of the pure, and it was a foregone conclusion that he would not long associate with such "unity." The Menshevik olive-branch to the "liquidators" was bad enough; far worse was the latters' refusal to be tempted back into the limbo of illegality and what they knew to be Lenin's projected sphere of influence. It was this "mess" that gave Lenin the pretext on which to start fighting again. Now he resolved that this unity must be dispersed and the only proper unity, that of a vigorous Bolshevik apparatus under his single control, must take its place.

His hostility was the greater for his having been forced through a personal ordeal. For it was at the Paris conference that the party as a whole had learned of his direct involvement in the great Tiflis robbery of 1907, and in consequence he had been forced to agree to burn the remaining banknotes. Also at the Paris Conference the episode of the Schmidt inheritance came to light and again Lenin had to agree to place the funds in the discretionary hands of three German trustees, Kautsky, Mehring and Klara Zetkin, though it would take eighteen months of intrigue, pressure and scandal to make him hand over even a part of the money. The fact that both factions may have wanted to control these funds for their own purposes did not diminish the propaganda value to the Mensheviks of Lenin's moral negligence.

In order to effect a final break Lenin resorted to his customary technique. His own agents, illegally despatched to Russia, were to establish their own commission and prepare the ground for a party conference. Throughout 1911 Lenin conducted his preparations. His aim, of convening a meeting that would proclaim Bolshevik principles and Bolshevik institutions in the name of the entire party, was greatly helped by the calculating intervention of the Tsarist secret police. Minutely informed by their own agents in the Bolshevik organisation, the police recognised in Lenin a wedge that would, they hoped, maintain the forces of Social Democracy in permanent dislocation and impotence.

Thus they ensured that, while Bolsheviks who were working for conciliation were arrested, Lenin's agents preparing for his conference were left in peace to complete their task. Yet Lenin's Russian Organising Commission failed almost totally to gain recognition among the local committees, even as representative of the Bolshevik faction, and as a result the "party" conference which convened in Prague in January 1912 was representative of no more than the fourteen voting delegates who attended it. Protests against calling the meeting a party conference were ignored by the Leninist majority, who went on to proclaim it the "All-party Conference of the RSDRP, and the supreme organ of the party." The legend is compounded in Soviet nomenclature as the "Sixth (Prague) All-Russian Conference of the RSDRP."

A new Central Committee was elected, comprising seven picked Bolsheviks including Lenin and his closest associate, Grigory Zinoviev, and one Roman Malinovsky, who was later to be exposed as a police spy.

In April 1912, having persuaded the Central Committee to withdraw its subsidy to Trotsky's *Pravda,* Lenin began to publish his own legal newspaper for the Russian workers. He appropriated the name of Trotsky's paper, *Pravda,* in the expectation that he would thus acquire the substantial good-will that it had built up. Lenin's policy was now to enter the same arena of legal operations as the Mensheviks and the "Liquidators" and to rival them for the allegiance of the workers. Influence over the legal labour movement and trade unions was to be achieved by clandestine cells under party control, which would be ready to direct the massed workers when the moment of insurrection returned. Lenin's renewed vigorous and attacking policy provoked his opponents to greater efforts at uniting their own forces.

But however mythical Lenin's claims to represent party opinion were, his opponents were not, nor it seems ever would be, sufficiently aggressive to compete with him for the new, and psychologically crucial, party titles that he had once again arrogated to his own faction. In August 1912, Trotsky, the most active "unifier," and the leading Mensheviks, organised a conference in Vienna which gave rise to a new configuration known as the August Bloc.

All shades of opinion attended, except that the Polish Social Democrats and Plekhanov were not represented, and Lenin did not deign to attend "their" conference. Among the non-Leninist Bolsheviks who did attend was one from Moscow who was in fact a police spy and whose secret assignment was to disrupt the proceedings.

Far more representative of party opinion than Lenin's "All-party Conference," the August meeting nonetheless described itself as no more than it really was, a "Conference of RSDRP Organisations." And, still on the defensive against Lenin, it called its Central Committee by the ephemeral title of Organising Committee. The extent of this error of judgement would fully emerge when, in competing with the Mensheviks for the workers' support, Lenin would be able to speak from the "official" platform, while the Mensheviks would have to expend their energies in staking their claim to legitimacy. Moreover, the very range of the "August Bloc" and the endemic dissidence of Russian socialists soon rendered the combination sterile as an organisational entity, and negligible as an apparatus to compare with the Bolsheviks.

In spite of these defects in the Menshevik leadership and in spite of the competitive attitude of the Bolsheviks, when the two factions fought the elections to the Fourth Duma, in September 1912, the Mensheviks gained seven and the Bolsheviks six seats. Such a nearly equal result was possible because the campaign was fought on a non-factional basis and, indeed, the workers were reluctant to distinguish Bolshevik from Menshevik. As well as the Mensheviks, any Bolsheviks, including most of the Bolshevik Duma deputies, would also have welcomed unity.

The relative autonomy of the Duma Social Democrats made it possible for them to give some rein to these feelings, and at the end of 1912 the two Duma groups agreed that they would henceforth act in accord. To his intense annoyance Lenin now found that the editors of *Pravda* (Stalin and Molotov) were making judicious cuts in his articles in order to attenuate his anti-Menshevik tone. Lenin acted quickly to open the eyes of both *Pravda* and "his" deputies and to redirect their view towards what they must consider their proper goal: a split in the Duma group and the separate conduct of the two factions within the Duma. The means at his disposal for effecting this strategem are more a comment on the regime that covertly abetted him than they are on Lenin, for he at any rate had never concealed duplicity as a valuable weapon.

Roman Malinovsky entered Lenin's ranks at the Prague Conference of 1912, where he also met his leader for the first time. He was already a salaried agent of the Tsarist secret police, which he had been serving certainly since 1909. His activities, apart from a criminal past, had to date consisted of organising and running the Petersburg Metal Workers' Union, where he diligently pursued the legal work of the good Menshevik he was then thought to be. Simultaneously, however, he abetted the interests of the state by withstanding Lenin's attempts to infiltrate his union, which, it seemed to the police, would involve a return to the old habits of the illegal underground. When the movement towards unity in the party seemed near success, Malinovsky was instructed to turn Bolshevik, and to work for a position close to Lenin. The unity of the party was fought against by the police, who observed that as long as the factions were mutually hostile the police could more easily keep them in their present state of impotence. And since Lenin was working tirelessly to-wards total disruption the police naturally sought to help him.

The policy of infiltrating agents into the Social Democratic party continued in spite of the great repercussions of the Socialist Revolutionary-Azef scandal in 1909. As long as the masses were quiescent the police calculated that the risk of further scandals was worth the opportunity to manipulate the levers of control at the very summit of the party. Thus in both factions police agents were helped to high positions of trust by the judicious and well-planned removal of local leaders. The Malinovsky card turned out to be an ace of trumps.

Lenin was enormously impressed by Malinovsky's energy and experience as a workers' leader. He put him up to run as a Social Democrat candidate for the elections to the Fourth Duma, and the police used their good offices to cover up Malinovsky's criminal past, which should have disqualified him. His candidacy was also safeguarded by the timely arrest of local contenders. His election was greeted by the police with a ten-fold increase in his salary, and by Lenin with his appointment as Duma spokesman for the Bolsheviks. The Social Democrat group as a whole chose him as its vice-chairman, with the Menshevik Chkheidze as chairman.

Malinovsky's role in the Duma was doubled by the police spy Chernomazov who became editor of the Bolshevik *Pravda*, in May 1913. Its conciliatory editor, Stalin, had been arrested in March as a direct result of a Malinovsky stratagem. Chernomazov followed Lenin's "splitting" line until February 1914, when he was "unmasked" by a police move calculated to deflect growing attention to Malinovsky.

By late 1913, however, Malinovsky and Lenin had succeeded in their common task, and the Social Democrat group in the Duma had been split into its factional components, with the six Bolsheviks claiming equal voice with the seven Mensheviks. Suspicion, which had existed from the very beginning of Malinovsky's Bolshevik career, was mounting rapidly. Now that his police role, of splitting the Duma group, was accomplished it was important for the police to reduce his stature as a spokesman of revolution. Also the mounting suspicion threatened to undo his police work, for nothing welded the factions so well as the discovery of sabotage. Therefore, in May 1914 Malinovsky suddenly, and without prior notice to anyone, resigned from the Duma on orders from the police, giving health reasons as his excuse.

He went to Lenin, who was living at Cracow, close to the Russian frontier. There he spun a yarn that his sudden resignation had been forced upon him by the police who threatened to expose him as a rapist. The rumours about Malinovsky that Lenin had previously succeeded in silencing, with threats of fire and brimstone, sprang to life with a vengeance and Lenin again vehemently defended his "wonderful workers' leader." The Mensheviks demanded a full party tribunal to examine the case. The possible outcome would have been more disastrous to Lenin than to the regime, and he evidently recognised this, for he evaded the Menshevik demand by forming a tribunal of his own.

The tribunal consisted of Lenin, Zinoviev and another "man of trust," Hanecki-Fürstenberg. It could not have been a less impartial body had it included Malinovsky himself. The culprit was exonerated and, as it was Lenin's habit to attack when cornered, the "tribunal" attacked the Mensheviks as treacherous calumniators. Malinovsky was admonished in the Bolshevik press for abandoning his post, and expelled from the party. During the First World War he was praised by the Bolsheviks for the valuable work he was doing,

under German auspices, to spread revolutionary propaganda among Russian prisoners-of-war. When he returned to Russia in November 1918, however, his full story had already been exposed by the opening of the police archives under the Provisional Government. Nonetheless Malinovsky demanded a hearing with Lenin's testimony. Lenin remained personally aloof, but a trial took place and Malinovsky was duly shot.

In 1914, Lenin made great public showing of his trust in Malinovsky and in his alibi. However, the possibility that the rumours were true alarmed him seriously. He wrote to Inessa Armand (in English); "Very improbable but we are obliged to control all 'ouï-dire' . . . You can easily imagine how much I am worried." A letter which he wrote to another Bolshevik deputy, in the early summer of 1914 when an investigation by the Socialist International was pending, reveals what he really felt about the man he so ardently defended. "We've finished with Malinovsky, it's all over. He's dead, suicide. No good nagging on about it and wasting time. To work, and down with the gutter journalists!" Malinovsky, though politically "dead," was in reality enjoying the 6,000-rouble retirement bonus his police chiefs had given him, and still very capable of compromising Lenin.

In the summer of 1914 the Socialist International intervened in the factional discord of the Russian party, offering its good offices as mediator. Lenin who was "extremely nervous, almost ill" would not attend the hearings in Brussels, but sent instead his confidante and friend, Inessa Armand. He impressed upon her that the Bolshevik "autonomous party" would not have its hands tied by any outside agency. She was to treat the International Bureau, which conducted the hearing, as no more than a mediator whose function was "to convey to the enemy: (1) our *terms* and (2) the *objective facts,* and that's all!!"

The conference produced a resolution which was as conciliatory as Lenin could have expected. It found that the differences within the Russian Social Democratic party were not substantial enough to hamper unity, and it called for unity on the basis of the party programme. A general unification congress should take place, and the minority must accept the view of the majority. The double irony here was that Lenin had no intention as the minor-ity of accepting the views of the majority, much less the exhortations of "that fool Kautsky," the chairman at the Socialist International hearing. He had already set in train the preparations for yet another, final, "party" congress at which the separate, autonomous existence of the Bolshevik party was to be proclaimed once and for all. In the event, both the projected "unification" and the Bolshevik congress were forestalled by the outbreak of the First World War.

The association of the word intelligentsia with radicalism in Russian history sometimes serves to obscure the fact that there were people of high education and intellectual talent loyal to the tsar. S. S. OLDENBURG (*ca.* 1885–1940) is an example. The son of a distinguished scholar who was permanent secretary of the Academy of Sciences, he had a wide range of interests, including Russian and foreign literature, the French Revolution, Chinese affairs and politics. Before the Revolution of 1917 Oldenburg was an active liberal, a member of the zemstvo of Tver province, and a constitutional monarchist by persuasion. Living abroad after 1917, he wrote a two-volume history entitled *The Reign of Emperor Nicholas II,* which was published by an obscure émigré monarchist association and has never received the attention that its careful research deserves.*

S. S. Oldenburg

Impressive Progress Since 1905

"One does not have to be a prophet to say that the year 1914 does not promise anything outstanding in our socio-political life," wrote V. D. Kuz'min-Karavaev, a well-known liberal political figure, in the New Year's survey in *Vestnik Evropy (The Herald of Europe).* Actually no appreciable change in the attitude of educated Russian society was externally noticeable. Russia, as Stolypin had accurately put it, was, as before, "dissatisfied with herself." In rural zemstvo and city council circles, which dominated the Duma, oppositional tendencies appeared again. Rumors were rife about coming limitations on the rights of popular government; there were sharp criticisms of the activities of various ministers,

especially N. A. Maklakov [internal affairs], I. G. Shcheglovitov [justice], L. A. Kasso [education], and V. K. Sabler [Holy Synod]. Disorder reigned in Right-wing circles, where different organizations, such as the League of the Archangel Michael, headed by V. M. Purishkevich, were much more preoccupied with settling scores with other Right-wingers than with "the struggle against revolution." A kind of grayness, an undefined, blind opposition, lacking clear slogans or goals, settled over political life. On New Year's Day, L. Tikhomirov wrote in *Moskovskii Vedomosti (The Moscow Gazette):*

The most alarming inertness is notable in present-day attitudes. Perhaps we live quietly, but

*From S. S. Oldenburg', *Tsarstvovanie Imperatora Nikolai II, tom II, chast'3, Dumskaia Monarkhiia 1907–1914 (The Reign of Emperor Nicholas II, vol. II, part 3, The Duma Monarchy 1907–1914)* (Munich: Izdatel'stvo obschshestva rasprostraneniia russkoi natsional'noi i patrioticheskoi literatury, 1949), pp 110–117, 120–123, 127–128. Translated by Robert H. McNeal.

it is a lifeless quietude. We not only do not see any passion for something great, idealistic, embracing the whole nation, but even the belief in the reality of something of this sort has evaporated. . . .

The political situation in Russia might seem unsatisfactory and even tense, yet at the same time the country was living a full life, which had little to do with the accusing speeches of the opposition politicians. In an interview with the editor of the *Berliner Tageblatt,* during a trip abroad in autumn of 1913 [Premier] V. N. Kovkovstov said of domestic discontent: "This may be true of the large cities, but a hundred kilometers from the large centers and thirty kilometers from the provincial capitals they know nothing of these politics." Although the Russian press replied sarcastically to these words, they were exceedingly close to the truth.

In the twentieth year of the reign of the emperor Nicholas II, Russia had achieved the highest level of material success that she had ever known. It was only five years after Stolypin had said, "Give us twenty years of peace, domestic and foreign, and you will not recognize present-day Russia," and the change had already begun to be felt. With bumper harvests in 1912 and 1913, the period from summer 1912 to summer 1914 saw the peak of achievement of the Russian economy. In twenty years the population of the empire had grown by fifty million persons—40 percent, a growth rate of over three million a year. The general standard of living rose appreciably at the same time, and the population was increasing, which testified to the vitality of the nation and the existence of conditions that made it possible to feed a growing number of people. The quantity of Russian and foreign goods that were consumed by the Russian market more than doubled in these twenty years. For example, the consumption of sugar rose from 8 pounds

per head in 1894 to over 18 pounds per head in 1913. Even though the sugar beet harvest failed in 1911–1912 and the price rose significantly, this did not cause a reduction in demand. Sugar had become a necessity to the broad mass of the populace. The growth of income from the alcoholic beverages monopoly (causing some criticism on moral grounds) testified to the rise in the standard of living. Beer production doubled and the consumption of spirits increased. Tea consumption increased from 40 million kilograms in 1890 to 75 million in 1913.

Thanks to the growth of agricultural production, the development of means of communication, and the prudent handling of food reserves, the "famine years" of the beginning of the twentieth century had become a thing of the past. Crop failure did not mean famine. A poor harvest in individual localities was taken care of by the production of other districts.

The bread-grains crop (rye, wheat, and barley), which was on the average somewhat under 36 million tons at the beginning of the reign, rose to over 74 million tons in 1913–1914. The composition of the crop changed to some extent: the wheat and barley crops doubled and the wheat crop nearly equaled the rye crop, whereas formerly rye alone had comprised nearly half the crop. Taking into account the growth of exports (about a fourth of Russian grain was exported) and the rise in population, the domestic consumption per capita indisputedly increased. In the cities the consumption of white bread began to rival that of black.

The quantity of manufactured goods consumed per capita doubled. Even though Russian textile production doubled, the importation of textiles also increased severalfold. Deposits in state savings banks rose from 300 million rubles in 1894 to two billion in 1913. The number of letters mailed rose from 400 million to two billion, and the number of telegrams rose from 60 million to 200 million per year.

Industrial production increased simultaneously with the flourishing of agriculture, not lagging behind the high growth rate of the first half of the reign. The decline in growth rate in the first years of the twentieth century gave way in 1909 to a new acceleration. Coal mining increased continually. The Donets Basin, which yielded less than 5.4 million tons in 1894, produced over 28 million tons in 1913. In the later years the exploitation of the mighty deposits of the Kuznets Basin in western Siberia began. Coal production of the whole empire increased fourfold in twenty years. Oil production in the old Baku field did not achieve its former level after the fires of 1905, but new sources on the Apsheron Peninsula [near Baku] and other places (Grozny, Emba) almost made good this loss, and in 1913 oil production again approached 10.8 million tons per year, two thirds more than at the beginning of the reign. The demand for fuel increased steadily as a result of industrial growth. In addition to oil, coal and wood (the oldest form of fuel, which was still the main fuel in the north and northeast of Russia), peat deposits were also exploited, and research was conducted on other combustible materials.

Following the opening of the rich iron deposits at Krivoi Rog (South Russia) and manganese at Nikopol and Chiaturi (Transcaucasia), the metallurgical industry grew rapidly. Pig iron production increased *fourfold* in twenty years; copper, *fivefold*. The extraction of manganese ore, most of which was shipped abroad, also increased fivefold.

If some kinds of machinery, especially factory equipment, were still imported, mainly from Germany, locomotives, railroad cars, and rails were all made in Russia. But there was also rapid growth in machine production in later years. The capital value of Russian machinery factories rose in *three years* (1911–1914) from 120 to 220 million rubles.

The textile industry grew rapidly, barely keeping pace with the still more rapidly growing demand. Cotton production, which was 256,500 tons in 1894, doubled by 1911 and was continuing to rise. Russia was becoming less and less dependent on imported raw cotton. As early as 1913 Turkestan cotton supplied half the needs of Russian factories. Since the beginning of the reign the Turkestan cotton harvest had increased *sixfold*. The linen, wool, and silk industries increased their output by 75.8 percent. The total number of workers in the textile industry rose from two to five million in twenty years.

The upsurge of the Russian economy was mighty and many-sided. The growth of agriculture and of the enormous domestic market was so powerful in the second decade of the reign that Russian industry did not reflect at all the industrial crisis of 1911–1912, which was a serious blow to Europe and America. Russia's growth continued unabated. Nor did the crop failure of 1911 halt the progress of the Russian economy.

The demand for agricultural machinery, household utensils, and decorative goods in rural Russia created competition between Russian and foreign (mainly German) industry, which unleashed a growing quantity of cheap goods on the Russian market. Inexpensive foreign goods were popular in rural Russia and made possible a rapid improvement in the standard of living there.

This mighty growth was reflected in the income of the treasury, which rose from 1.2 billion rubles at the beginning of the reign to 3.5 billion. More than half of this revenue came from the liquor monopoly and the state-owned railroads. Year after year the government's receipts exceeded expenditures, and there was ready cash on hand. For over ten years, 1904–1913, the excess revenue over expenditures was more than 2 billion rubles. The gold reserves rose from 648 million rubles in 1894 to 1,604 million in 1914.

The state budget grew without the introduction of new taxes or increase of old ones, reflecting the growth of the national economy. The increase in traffic on state railroads, the liquor trade, taxed sales of tobacco and sugar, taxes on industry and customs revenues—all this meant that the national income grew faster than the state budget. The length of the rail system and of telegraph lines doubled since 1894, as did the size of the river-transport fleet, which was the largest in the world.

The Russian army grew approximately in proportion to the population. In 1914 it comprised 37 corps, not counting Cossacks [about fifty regiments] and irregular units, with a peacetime establishment of over 1.3 million men. After the Japanese war the army was basically reorganized. The chief of the German General Staff, General von Moltke, in a report of February 24, 1914, in the name of the secretary of state for foreign affairs, von Jagow, made the following appraisal of the reforms in the army during 1907–1913: "The military preparedness of Russia since the Russo-Japanese War has achieved entirely exceptional success and is now at a high point that has not been achieved previously. It follows that one should note in particular that in some respects it exceeds the military preparedness of other powers including Germany...."

Foreigners took note of the transformation that was taking place in Russia. At the end of 1913, the editor of *Economist Europien,* Edmund Théry, was commissioned by two French ministries to investigate the Russian economy. Noting the startling success in all fields, Théry concluded; "If the state of the European nations from 1912 to 1950 continues as it has from 1900 to 1912, Russia will by the middle of the present century dominate Europe both in political and economic-financial respects." ...

Maurice Baring, the well-known English writer who had spent several years in Russia and knew the country well, wrote in his book *The Mainsprings of Russia* (spring 1914), "There has perhaps never been a period when Russia was more materially prosperous than at the present moment, or when the great majority of the people seemed to have so little obvious cause for discontent." Baring, observing the oppositional mood in educated society, noted, "The casual inquirer, glancing at the subject for the first time, will be tempted to ask, 'What more can the Russian people want?'" Conscientiously presenting the viewpoint of intelligentsia circles, Baring noted that discontent was widespread mainly *among the upper classes,* while "the population on the whole are prosperous at the present moment, and their grievances are neither sharp nor strong enough, nor sufficiently abundant, to make the temperature of their discontent rise to the boiling point."

The material side [of Russian life in 1914] is most often mentioned because it was so strikingly apparent. But perhaps the progress of public education was still more important. "One portentous feature stands out more and more prominently— public education is growing mightily," wrote I. Zhilkin, the leader of the Trudovik group in the First Duma, in November 1913. "Unheard, almost unnoticed, a tremendous achievement is coming about: Russia is passing from illiteracy to literacy ...." The following figures testify to the growth of public education: in 1914 the government, zemstovs, and city councils spent about 300 million rubles on education (in 1894 it was about 40 million). E. P. Kovalevsky, the *rapporteur* in the Duma on the budget of the ministry of education, stated on June 6, 1914, that by January 1, 1915, universal education would be achieved in 51 districts; by 1920 in 218 districts (out of 800 districts). The number of pupils enrolled on January 1, 1912, already exceeded eight million (out of about fourteen million of school age). According to Kovalevsky's data, there were 80,000 persons enrolled in institutions of higher learning (40,000 of which were in universities). There were 700,000 enrolled in high schools and about 50,000 in trade or lower technical schools. On the initiative of the Third Duma, the principle was adopted of increasing the education budget by 20 million rubles each year (10 million to build new schools, 10 million for their maintenance). In 1912 there were 122 teachers' colleges, with 20,000 students.

Dismissing political fears of the consequences, the government was granting a large "credit" to the intelligentsia in the matter of education. But while retaining some supervision to try to prevent openly revolutionary propaganda in schools, the government at the same time went along with the initiative of the State Duma, zemstovs, and city councils in the matter of establishing universal education. . . .

The unparalleled speed with which cooperatives grew reflected the spontaneous economic activity of the mass of the populace. Up to 1897 there were only about a hundred consumer co-ops with a small membership, and a few hundred small credit unions. In 1897 standard statutes for consumer cooperatives, which could be opened merely with the consent of the local authorities, were issued. [Before 1905 all types of associations, even social clubs, usually could be formed only with the permission of the central government.] In the same year the first credit unions with which the government or zemstvos collaborated were formed. Even by 1905 about a thousand consumer cooperatives and 1500 credit unions had been formed, but the real flowering of cooperatives began only after 1906. Both consumer co-ops and small scale credit unions spread from the cities to the countryside. By January 1, 1912, there were almost 7000 consumer cooperatives, a *sixfold* increase in *five years,* and rural co-ops, whose number had increased twelvefold, constituted two-thirds of the total.

Some cooperatives (for example, the Society of Transbaikal Railroad Employees) had a turnover in the millions of rubles. In 1914 the Moscow Union of Consumers' Societies merged 800 cooperatives, with an annual turnover of 10.5 million rubles, and was the fifth largest union of cooperatives in Europe. In 1914 credit unions had seven times more capital than in 1905 and had nine million members. Credit unions contributed 85 percent of the capital of the Moscow People's Bank, which opened in 1912, and this gave a fresh impetus to the development of co-ops.

The growth of cooperatives created a demand for semiintellectual work. A new social stratum, which like school teachers was "popular socialist" [peasant-oriented socialists] in its theoretical outlook, was created. But theory had little effect on the practical activity of cooperatives; in general they shunned "pure politics." There was even a special ideology appearing among them, which endowed cooperation with universal significance. Cooperation was to reform all economic relationships, to abolish "exploitation," and to found a people's economy on the basis of all-embracing humanitarianism.

The government did not hinder the development of cooperatives (as was sometimes claimed when individual cooperative workers were arrested for revolutionary propaganda). On the contrary, the widespread collaboration of the government enabled credit unions to grow rapidly. The State Bank lent hundreds of millions of rubles to small credit organizations. "In no other country, possibly excepting India, did credit cooperatives enjoy such government support as in Russia," a well-known cooperative worker wrote afterward.

A new Russia was emerging. Political speeches were still embellished with the words "reaction," "stagnation," "paralysis of the governmental organism." But the facts contradicted these phrases, which were becoming too rhetorical. All foreigners were starting to ignore them.

At the end of 1913 an article by Prince E. N. Trubetskoi [a liberal] appeared in *Russkaia Mysl'* (*Russian Thought*). "Two new facts in particular strike the observer of the Russian countryside in recent years," he wrote, "the rise of the standard of material welfare and the astonishing growth of a new social order." The improvement of technique, the rise in the cost of labor, the appearance of city clothing (from tortoise-shell combs to galoshes and umbrellas) among the peasants—all this runs parallel to the striking growth of rural cooperatives. And this growth did not occur in opposition to the state, but with its direct material support. "The government did not spare on funds to aid zemstvos in all measures that were devoted to the betterment of the peasants' welfare. . . . What seemed impossible in 1905 had been accomplished." . . . On this basis Trubetskoi concluded that the old "Pugachev" socialism had been left behind, that in Russia peasant landholders formed a basis for "bourgeois democracy."

"Yes," answered an eminent narodnik [agrarian socialist] publicist, I. I. Bunakov, "the rise in peasant welfare, in connection with agricultural technique and the development of peasant society, mainly in the form of cooperative organizations, is a profound social transformation on the Russian countryside, which, so wrongly, is nearly ignored by our urban intelligentsia . . . In these years of so-called 'reaction' and 'stagnation' there has been on the Russian countryside—and consequently for the basic mass of the Russian social order—an improvement, the significance of which must be immense for the future of the country." . . .

"Are there such sudden metamorphoses in history?" While doubting the durability of the new trend in the countryside, Bunakov at least did not deny that it existed, and he examined it attentively.

The rank and file of the intelligentsia in general refused to see it and, as before, regarded Russian reality only as "oppression," "arbitrariness," "poverty," "the suppression of all spontaneity." P. B. Struve [an intellectual Marxist turned liberal] commented on this in *Russkaia Mysl'* in March 1914, in an article entitled, "Why Has Our Spiritual Life Stagnated?" He mentioned that formerly the ideas of the intelligentsia had run ahead of the Russian actuality, but now, on the contrary, "Life steadily, with elemental force, moves forward and ideological work lags hopelessly behind, producing nothing, marking time."

What caused this phenomenon? The intelligentsia has lost faith in its former ideals. It already doubted materialism, the ideals of the eighteenth and nineteenth centuries, even the all-redeeming significance of the revolution, but *it had not decided to admit this to itself.* Meanwhile, this disillusionment went deep. It was reflected in the younger generation, in students, even in youths who were only beginning to live. "The authority of the older generation has fallen even lower in the eyes of the young than is customary among fathers and children. . . . It has been a long time since it has sunk as low in Russia as it has in these years of political and moral crisis," wrote Professor V. I. Vernadsky in the *Annual* of the Kadet newspaper *Rech' (Speech)* in 1914.

The decline of the old intelligentsia beliefs gave rise to a wave of suicides among young participants around 1910. This wave then began to recede and to be replaced by religious searchings. In the institutions of higher learning, where politics were in a frozen state (not so much because of the repressive measures of Kasso as because of the change in mood of the students), various religious circles (an unheard-of phenomenon) began to appear. In 1913 for the first time Russian students participated in the congress of the world organization of Christian youth in the United States. . . .

A new feature of a wholly different sort was the awakening interest in all kinds of sports. Previously, serious Russian youths considered sport to be a "nonintelligentsia" occupation. Now soccer and tennis clubs sprang up everywhere. Gymnastic organizations for children and youths began to become widespread. One was named the *poteshnye* after the first play-soldier comrades of Peter the Great and was occupied with a kind of preservice military training. Another was the "Sokol," a Slavic sports organization that was most highly developed among the Czechs. And there were the Boy Scouts of the English kind.

The emperor followed the development of these organizations with special interest, especially the *poteshnye*. He donated 10 million rubles to them from monies that were within his discretion and proposed to create a special government department of physical education. But Kokovtsov said that the Duma scarcely wanted to grant credits for the new department in this question (as in the question of the organi-

zation of a special ministry of health) the Duma lagged appreciably behind the initiative of the government. . . .

In 1914 Russia was much less poisoned by politics than in 1904. The political parties had exceedingly little significance. As before, the Kadets were the party of the intelligentsia. The Octobrists were the party of the zemstvo leaders; the industrialists in the later years transferred their allegiance from the Octobrists to the Progressivists. The more Right-wing movements were not composed of any definite social stratum (except perhaps the landed nobility), but found many adherents among the mass of the Russian populace, mainly urban folk in the western regions.

The socialist-Marxists (Social Democrats) exercised a significant influence on the workers and had, if you will, a more developed party organization, even though they did not exist "legally." The socialist-narodniks (Socialist Revolutionaries, Trudoviks, and Popular Socialists) had many adherents among the rural quasi-intelligentsia. But, with the possible exception of the Social Democrats, not one party developed a widespread, planned propaganda program.

Neither the intelligentsia, which had lost confidence in its old faith and had not found a new one, nor the primitive-socialist quasi-intelligentsia, possessed political experience or a broad, statesmanlike outlook. As before, in the midst of this formless "public" only the tsarist authority, based on a strong tradition and long experience in ruling, which had experienced cadres to carry out its projects, could direct the life of the complex country. Only authority which stood outside and above the interests of separate groups and strata in the country could carry out basic reforms, as is shown by the case of the [agrarian reform] law of November 9, 1906 [which was initiated by the government in 1906

and passed by the Duma only in 1909].
The legislative institutions could serve the
government not so much as a foundation
as an occasional *brake,* and also as a mea-
suring device to show the "temperature"
or the "barometric pressure" of the country. . . . The emperor did not at this time
consider it possible to increase the influence of "the public" on the course of affairs
of state. He did not see in the Duma, or in
Russian society in general, those elements
to which the Imperial Authority *would have
the right to delegate the destiny of Russia.*

In 1964 Leopold Haimson challenged the optimistic appraisal of the condition of the Russian Empire in an essay entitled "The Problem of Social Stability in Urban Russia, 1905–1917," which stresses the increasing alienation and violence of the industrial workers. Among the numerous responses to this provocative article, that of HANS ROGGER (b. 1923) of the University of California, Los Angeles, is notable for its breadth and cogency. He comes to the study of this problem with a special knowledge of one of the main foundations of the imperial regime: Russian nationalism. Rogger began his work in this field with the book *National Consciousness in Eighteenth Century Russia* and then shifted his focus to the early twentieth century and the Right-wing nationalists of Russia, writing several articles on the subject. This theme is developed on a broader scale in his essay in the anthology he edited in collaboration with Eugene Weber, *The European Right.**

Hans Rogger

The Question Remains Open

To speak of Russia in 1914 means, inevitably, to think of it in the light of 1917. The magnitude of what happened in the later year—and even more what was to follow—overshadows the events of the last six months of peace Russia was to know for a long time. Yet they were agitated months, and whatever inclination there may be for nostalgia to invest them with the bitter-sweet of lost hopes or the glamour of a happier age, there is remarkably wide agreement that Russia in 1914 was in the throes of an internal crisis which might assume revolutionary proportions. The re- collections of survivors—in which most often the last few pre-war years merge to form one general impression—are borne out by contemporary evidence. Disagreement concerns rather the nature and the probable outcome of the crisis, and the potential of the war for making inevitable or avoiding, speeding up or retarding, the country's decline into political and social disintegration. In order to attempt some answer to these questions it may be useful to cut across the usual chronological boundaries in order to see what Russian society's response to the war can tell us of its

*From Hans Rogger, "Russia in 1914," *Journal of Contemporary History*, vol. 1, no. 4 (October, 1966), pp. 95–103, 114–119. Copyright © 1966, The Institute of Contemporary History. Reprinted by permission of Harper & Row, Publishers and George Weidenfeld and Nicolson, Ltd.

likely reactions to the internal crisis which war, temporarily, reduced to secondary importance.

The Russian crisis was three-fold: political, social, and spiritual (or cultural); its most visible part, as 1914 opened, was the political one. "Long before the war," Fedor Stepun recalled, "all politically conscious people lived as on a volcano," a sentiment which was in 1914 no longer confined to the liberal or radical opposition. "We live on a volcano," wrote the arch-conservative and chauvinistic *Kievlianin* in April, noting "sharp displeasure with the present regime" even on the part of the absolutely loyal classes of society. This displeasure, although it stemmed from different sources, was noticeable also on the far right of the political spectrum, where there was fear that 1905 might be enacted all over again, and the opposition recover the unity it had then displayed and quickly lost.

Crisis had, of course, been endemic in Russian political life for some time; in heightened form at least since the assassination of Stolypin in 1911. Its intensification in early 1914 was due to actual and feared changes in government policy and personnel, changes which seemed to make a purely political solution of the crisis ever more difficult. The most dramatic of these was the sudden dismissal, at the end of January, of the Chairman of the Council of Ministers, Kokovtsev, who, although his popularity in the country at large and among the opposition in particular, had hardly been great, appeared now to be the last defender of Stolypin's legacy: qualified cooperation with the legislature in the work of constructive reform. His leaving, and the manner of it ("He was let go like a domestic," one of the Grand Dukes observed), was widely interpreted as a victory for the forces of reaction. These had gained

influence at court, would now dominate the government and use their new-won power to destroy what was left of the Stolypin compromise, and assume towards the Duma, the non-Russian nationalities and the working-class movement harsh and irreconcilable policies. "A fire is burning under a relatively calm surface," reported an Austrian diplomat, "an unskilled hand may fan the flames and start a conflagration if the nationalist hotheads, together with the extreme Right, bring about a union of the oppressed nationalities and the socialist proletariat."

There were several members of the government who qualified for a *testimonium paupertatis* as far as their political skills were concerned. Shcheglovitov, the Minister of Justice, who had let the [antisemitic] Beilis ritual murder case come to trial, was constantly infringing the rights of the judiciary and the bar and had used his office to render interpretations of the law which disqualified "undesirable" electors and candidates. L. A. Kasso, the Minister of Education, besides harassing students and professors, blocked expansions of educational opportunity proposed by the Duma. The new head of government, I. L. Goremykin, was a relic of former days, remembered mainly for his struggles with the first Duma in 1906; his appearance before the fourth led to lengthy disturbances in the house. Above all, there was N. A. Maklakov, the Minister of the Interior and imperial favourite, who had made no secret of his sympathies for the parties of the extreme Right and was believed to favour a revision of the Fundamental Laws (tantamount to a coup d'état) which would convert the legislative institutions granted in 1905 into purely consultative bodies.

No coup took place, but while the Duma sat in the spring of 1914, signs multiplied that the government was deter-

mined to whittle away its rights of interpellation, of legislative initiative, and even
of immunity for statements made from the
rostrum of the lower house. The "constitutional opposition," consisting of about 100
Constitutional Democrats (Kadets) and
Progressists, and the Left (24 "Labourites"
and Social-Democrats) were joined in
some of their protests by members who sat
to their right—primarily, Octobrists and
Centrists. In discussing appropriations for
the Ministry of the Interior, this opposition
succeeded for the first time in the history of
the Duma in rejecting a specific portion of
the government's budget for the purpose of
political protest, while by a majority of 186
to 95, it criticized the Ministry for arbitrary restrictions on the activities of local
government, for provoking dissatisfaction
and disturbances among peaceful sections
of the population (i.e., the subject nationalities), and for not carrying out what was
called (presumably with tongue in cheek)
the Emperor's desire for fruitful collaboration between the executive and the legislature. The Ministry's policies, it was said,
threatened the tranquillity and the safety
of the nation. Just before it rose in June,
the Duma did, however, accept the government's military programme (earning
the Tsar's praise for its patriotism), but it
also voted an amendment to the state budget which forbade ministries from expend-
ing at their discretion unused sums assigned for specific purposes. The amendment was rejected by the Council of State
whose appointed members helped to make
the upper chamber a graveyard for liberal
hopes. . . .

With the legislature adjourned and the
confrontation between the government and
the opposition once more postponed, attention shifted to the social crisis which the
political one had partially reflected and
partly obscured. This reached its height
with the massive strikes and disorders
which took place in the industrial quarters
of St Petersburg during the visit of President Poincaré in early July, raged for
more than a week, required the use of
troops to keep them out of the centre of
town, and revealed a degree of aggressive-
ness and exasperation on the part of the
workers for which even sympathetic observers were unprepared. There had already
been so many strikes during the year, commented a writer for the Kadet newspaper
Rech, and they were due to so many different causes, that there was at first no
reason to attach any special importance to
this one. But although the number of
strikes and strikers in July was greater
than for any previous month of 1914, their
determination (or desperateness) was not
altogether new. . . .

The Austrian chargé d'affaires (Count
Czernin) was more perceptive when he
attributed the extent and violence of the
July days to the treatment the workers had
received at the hands of the police and
predicted that such means could only postpone, not avert, the threat of an explosion.
"If one continues to cling to such a senseless principle and keeps all safety-valves
closed, it can happen that the revolutionary organization of Russia will be completed before her military one." It is certain that German gold played no role in
the summer of 1914. It is less certain to
what extent the rebuilding of revolutionary organizations shattered in the years after 1906 was responsible for the intransigence of the workers. Badaev, a Bolshevik
Duma deputy, believed that even if they
had not been interrupted by the war, the
July demonstrations might not have led to
the decisive point of the revolutionary
struggle, for lockouts, mass arrests, and de-
portations had diminished the economic
strength and weakened the political organization of the working class, making necessary a respite for the regrouping of its

forces. Indeed, the Petersburg party committee of the Bolsheviks realized before the
workers did that their strike was bound to
be defeated and called on them to return
to work.

As early as April the political commentator of *Russkoe Bogatstvo* had written in his
monthly survey that, besides the conflict
being played out between government and
opposition in the Duma, the country at
large was full of combustible material of a
less controlled, less controllable, and more
elemental nature. "In particular, it seems
that the activism of the working masses is
beginning to outgrow the organizational
capabilities and possibilities of the working-
class intelligentsia." He, too, compared
the situation to the building up of pressures in a hermetically sealed boiler, pressures which had reached a degree of intensity sufficient to inspire the stokers (the
authorities) with fear of the consequences
of a further increase.

Those of the stokers who showed an
awareness of the seriousness of the social
crisis did not ascribe it to the efforts either
of German or even primarily of Russian
instigators. In a remarkable memorandum
which he submitted to the Tsar in February, P. N. Durnovo, a reactionary
member of the Council of State and former
Minister of the Interior, gave warning of
the danger of social revolution in case of
war. Although his prescience was due at
least as much to fear as to insight, he saw
clearly that the political and the social crisis were quite distinct and that the latter
was the more threatening. A political revolution, lacking broad support, was impossible; a social revolution, in a country
where the masses were unconsciously, almost instinctively, socialist, was not. "The
Russian masses, whether workmen or peasants, are not looking for political· rights,
which they neither want nor comprehend.
The peasant dreams of obtaining a gratu-

itous share of somebody else's land; the
workman, getting hold of the entire capital
and profits of the manufacturer."

Durnovo's definition of socialism may
have been faulty; his appraisal of the mass
mood and of the relationship between the
two crises was not. It was shared by the
Minister of Agriculture, Krivoshein, who
had the reputation of being a moderate,
perhaps even a liberal. He did not deny,
speaking in May, that radical propaganda
played its part in agitating the masses, but
viewed its authors as helpless to guide the
revolution which would surely come if
Russia went to war. It would be not so
much a revolution as a *pogrom,* a senseless,
pitiless, anarchic rising which would make
victims even of those who had conjured it
up.

The cultural crisis is seen as stemming
from similar perceptions on the part of
thoughtful men who felt that there was an
air of unreality, of impermanence, to all
the busy building and planning—political
and economic—in which their countrymen
were engaged. They, too, feared that
whatever gains had been made or were
still possible could all too easily be swept
away by the mighty floods of popular resentment that were barely restrained by
the feeble dikes of civilization and a decay-
ing state. The intelligentsia had to admit
to themselves that in the higher culture
which they were developing and which
was giving Russia a standing in the world,
the masses had no share, and that they
would probably sweep it away if given a
chance. The cultural elite felt keenly the
lack of contact with a people roused to
anger and violence. [The poet] Alexander
Blok's diaries are often cited to convey a
sense of the "deep uneasiness that was
gnawing at the loftiest and more sensitive
minds," an uneasiness which was taken to
indicate a loss of faith in the efficacy and

benefits of progress. Stepun derided the facile optimism of the enlightened, their belief in the possibility of controlling men and events, mocked their conceit that a happy resolution of Russia's crisis could be the work of a mere handful of politicians, a matter of reformed ministries and parliaments. In Andrei Bely's vision (*Petersburg*, 1913), the Russia of the father (imperial and bureaucratic) and the Russia of the son (revolutionary, intellectual, and visionary) are both doomed, as is the city in which their confused struggle is carried on.

For others, like the Kadet jurist I. V. Gessen, the crisis expressed itself in a feeling of fatigue and exhaustion, with the old guard of the intelligentsia still carrying on its work of political and cultural enlightenment by mere reflex and the younger generation losing itself in aesthetic innovation or sexual pursuits. The right-wing publicist and repentant revolutionary Lev Tikhomirov, spoke on 1 January 1914 of a most alarming inertia as the characteristic contemporary mood. "Perhaps we are living quietly. But this tranquillity is lifeless. Not only is there no striving for greatness or for ideals that could carry along the whole nation; belief itself in such an impulse has died out." Even many of those who did not share the cultural despair or sense of moral dissolution seemed afflicted by a spiritual malaise that made them question the meaning of their political or educational activities in the face of constant and often petty irritations on the part of government.

These irritations and annoyances were cumulatively disheartening and debilitating, but were they capable of becoming rallying cries for revolution in the face of apathy or indifference on the part of much of society, especially in the provinces, and, above all, in the face of the gulf of hostility, fear, or incomprehension which divided

the political opposition of the educated from the anger of the urban masses and the sullen discontent of the peasantry? Russia, as Stolypin had once put it, was dissatisfied with herself, she was morbidly irritable, on edge, full of symptoms of a deep-rooted distemper, but was she ready to translate irritation, dissatisfaction, uneasiness, into a revolutionary onslaught on the tsarist regime? And would the country follow the political opposition of "society" in such an onslaught?

There could be no certainty on that point, for Russians might well ask whether their crisis was one of growth or of decay. Which was the truer reflection of Russian reality? The political crisis, the prospect of another 1905 with the country united against the government? The social crisis, with the urban working class embittered alike by official persecution and what it felt to be unofficial indifference? Or was it the evidence of progress and improvement in the economy, in education, in the activity of local governments and agricultural cooperatives? Was there not reason to expect that political stagnation and social hostility would in time be overcome by the massive weight of the changes taking place in an expanding economy and society? Would not the political opposition, embracing ever more of the central portion of the political spectrum, carry the day over the government because it was supported by the general trend of the country's social and intellectual evolution? Might not the government retreat once more from an untenable position and yield to the moderate demands and aspirations of the vast majority of well-meaning, educated Russians, as Baron Rosen and others were urging it to do in order to forestall explosions from below?. . .

The political crisis, which loomed so large in the eyes of contemporaries, was probably most readily susceptible of settlement. The attitude taken after July by the liberal and moderate opposition to the government suggests that the gulf between them was perhaps not unbridgeable, that an accommodation with at least part of the opposition was possible, and that it might have been achieved by relatively minor concessions on the part of the administration. The positions of the contestants look less rigid than appeared to be the case before July, with neither side as determined or unified as talk of an impending clash would lead one to believe. The reactionaries in the cabinet and their adherents had no love for the Duma, and would gladly have done without it. Yet neither before nor during the war was there enough resolution or confidence among them to dismiss it or, for that matter, ideological commitment to such a course. Maklakov, believed most favourable to such action, had recoiled from it; nor was it impossible that he and other reactionary ministers might be sacrificed in case of need, as was to happen in 1915.

The appointment of Goremykin, taken at the time to be symbolic of the government's hostility to representative institutions, was thought by many observers to be purely temporary. It was widely expected that the Minister of Agriculture, Krivoshein, would shortly replace him and that he would heed the Tsar's injunction (contained in a rescript to Goremykin) to unify the cabinet and seek collaboration with the Duma. Krivoshein was said to be a liberal and popular in Duma circles, or a conservative who saw the need for cooperation with society. It is difficult to fix his political allegiances, or even to determine whether he had any, but his reputation and the fact that he was careful to maintain contact with the opposition created expectations that by July he would

initiate a more liberal course and pacify the critics. . . .

Lack of unity and of a unified political complexion in the government make it possible to envisage a change of course for the better. Lack of unity on the part of the opposition creates doubt that the only way out of the impasse between the state power and public opinion was either a revolution or a reactionary coup. The Tsar, while making no secret in private of his irritation with the parliamentary opposition, continued to declare in public his commitment to the reforms of 1905. This presented his political opponents with insuperable difficulties in achieving unity among themselves and their followers. A call for full adherence to the October Manifesto and the Fundamental Laws would not have been enough to assure joint action with the revolutionaries, while there was disagreement even among the Kadets as to how far or how hard one should push for such a goal. They were not prepared to cut all ties to the cabinet, as is shown by their participation in secret meetings on the defence budget from which the Left was excluded. And chances of converting the two anti-government votes of the spring into a more permanent opening to the Right were almost nonexistent. The Duma's right wing (some 150 deputies) could be counted upon to be subservient to whatever ministry was in power; a portion of the Centre group and the Octobrists (perhaps 100 members in all) were satisfied with the status quo, while a third group, consisting of Octobrists, some Progressists, and right-wing Kadets, were ready to settle for the "regime of the 3rd of June" (i.e. 1905 as amended and restricted by Stolypin) if only the government gave some sign of moderating its conduct. This left only the main body of the Kadets and Progressists in principled opposition. This was the "responsible" opposition (as Miliukov called it), which was supposedly capable of trying conclusions with the government, of engaging it in a contest from which one or the other would have had to emerge the victor. Even with the support of the Left (28 deputies) this was not likely. The Duma opposition lacked unity and strength and if its growth in early 1914 foreshadowed the Progressive Bloc of 1915, the latter also showed by its moderation what the price of unity would be.

As far as the wider opposition of society is concerned, it too looks less formidable from a post-July perspective, with as much political lethargy or indifference as there was of conscious disturbance or sympathy for the opposition parties. Miliukov himself, who had viewed the anti-government votes in the Duma as some kind of turning point, in September looked upon the war as a boon for having shaken the public out of its political apathy. The quick rally to the side of the regime in July 1914 by most of the educated public is no guarantee that the political crisis *would* have been settled; the further conduct of court and cabinet suggest rather the opposite. It does indicate, however, that it *could* have been settled with a little more intelligence and flexibility on the part of the administration. In that sense it *was* human folly that made revolution inevitable, not the clash of immovable forces and determined antagonists.

Taking reactions to the war as a starting point, one must conclude that the social crisis would have been vastly more difficult to compose than the political one. Even if they had been possessed of greater tact and skill, Russia's rulers would have found it difficult with the means at hand to remove the grievances of workers and peasants with speed, and without deepening the political crisis by infringing the economic interests of the privileged classes. There are numerous indications that the militancy of the urban working classes had outrun the organizational capabilities of the leftist leaders, and mass discontent was bound to increase with the burdens imposed by war. The splits which developed among socialist politicians over the issue of the war reflect their own uncertainty about the mood of the masses, with those remaining in Russia (and presumably possessed of a greater awareness of what that mood was) more opposed to the war than those abroad. The factory elections of September 1915, although later reversed, demonstrate how deepseated was worker distrust of authority and privilege.

Nor, as Mr. Haimson has reminded us,[1] is there a basis for confidence that a non-revolutionary trade-unionism could have directed the workers' resentment into safe reformist channels. While trade unions became legal in 1906, they continued to be harassed by the police, restricted to the purely local level, opposed by the majority of employers, numerically weak and incapable therefore of offering the best means for improving the workers' social and economic position. In spite of the improvement in money and real wages since 1909, industrial wages remained at a level that was barely adequate to meet the basic necessities of food, shelter, and clothing. Any continued improvement in the non-agricultural sector of the economy which would not have been matched by a very substantial improvement in wages would only have underscored for the workers their continued exclusion from the general prosperity. . . .

Reliable information about peasant attitudes and conduct is scarce on the ground and often contradictory, ranging from statements about the increasing frequency of disturbances in the years 1910–14 to es-

---

[1] "The Problem of Urban Stability in Russia, 1905–1917," *Slavic Review*, vol. 23, no. 4; vol. 24, no. 1.

timates of their marked decline during these same years. It does not seem likely, however, that the Stolypin reform could have furnished the answer to peasant unrest in a reasonable period of time.

A reform which may require 100 (Kutler) or even 40 to 45 years (Hoetzsch) for its work of pacification has doubtful title to that name, especially if its authors expect during its execution to be freed of disturbances which it is designed to correct. . . .

The response which Russia's cultural elite made to the war was another revelation of the chasm that divided it from the urban and rural masses. It tells us little, however, about the spiritual malaise which was supposedly but another dimension of Russia's political and social crisis. No artist or intellectual can be indifferent to the tremors by which his environment is shaken. He may, indeed, register them more sensitively than most of his contemporaries. But what he makes of his perceptions in his art or thought, and how immediate a reflection his work is of social or political reality, is another and most complicated matter. The hallmark of Russian culture in its Silver Age was precisely its rich diversity, and any attempt to classify it as either optimistic or pessimistic would do it violence. The facts of biography, of inner feelings, may well be as important here as those of history, of outer forces, and it is only the examination of their interplay in many individual instances that would justify an attempt at summary judgments. Even then, the evidence will not always be conclusive, as the case of Blok, for example, indicates. There are his diaries for the years 1911 to 1913; but there is also his confident poem "The New America" (dated 12 December 1913) with its vision of Russia transformed. It is doubtful, moreover, that cultural despair (where it existed) was a specifically Russian rather than a general European phenomenon, for no country's "high" culture was more finely attuned to universal currents and expressions than that of Russia. After all, even America, that model of robust hope, had its "cataclysmic thinkers." This is not to argue that the study of thought and letters furnishes no clues to the temper of an epoch or people. But these must be used with care and avoid a too rigid synchronization of political, social, and cultural phenomena.

It is possible, therefore, to view the spiritual or cultural crisis (if there was one) in a larger, European context, and not as a necessary outgrowth of Russia's social and political difficulties. As for the latter, it appears that the political opposition of the classes lacked coherence, that it would not join forces with the disaffected masses, and that their mutual alienation robbed the classes of confidence while confirming the masses in their hostility to all of privileged society, including its liberal sector. Under such circumstances, there was little prospect of a common front against tsarism which could exact true political liberty and representative government. Nor, for its part, did reaction have enough strength or confidence to impose a solution. Regarding the social crisis, Mr. Haimson may be right in saying that, even without war, the possibility existed of a radical overturn of the kind Russia was to experience in October 1917. But in order to judge of its probability, one would have to know the relative strength of the forces available and ready to make use of or to resist the social explosion which made October possible. In the course of such an inquiry, one might discover still other possible issues to the Russian crisis, issues which would have brought neither a major advance towards constitutional government nor the outburst of peasant and worker violence that 1917 was to witness.

Suggestions for Additional Reading

The student of history seeking to find his way in the ever-expanding maze of publications is well advised to keep in mind two general aids that are quite comprehensive and usually within a year or so of being up to date: (1) the book reviews and current check-list of articles in *The American Historical Review* and (2) *Historical Abstracts,* which is an indexed guide, with summaries, of articles only.

Concerning Russia in particular, the most convenient guide to books and articles for students of Russia in 1905–1914 is David M. Shapiro, (ed.), *A Select Bibliography of Works in English on Russian History 1801–1917* (Oxford, Basil Blackwell, 1962). Paul L. Horecky is the general editor of two fundamental bibliographical aids: *Basic Russian Publications, An Annotated Bibliography on Russia and the Soviet Union* (Chicago, 1962), which covers books in Russian, (see especially Part IV, History) and *Russia and the Soviet Union; A Bibliographic Guide to Western Language Publications* (Chicago, 1965; see especially Part VI, History).

The problem of Russia's development in 1905–1914 is treated in any general survey of Russian history, of which there are too many to list here, although the views expressed in such books are by no means without interest. However, there are not so many important books that focus on the century preceding 1914, and these must be of special interest for the light they cast on the problem discussed in the present book, and its immediate antecedents. The most ambitious of these is Hugh Seton-Watson, *The Russian Empire 1801–1917* (New York, 1967). Here the reader may find much information, presented with judicious detachment. Since there is no important comprehensive study of the nationality problem in the late Russian empire, (a topic of potentially great consequence for the

destiny of the empire), Seton-Watson's summation of this question is an especially valuable feature of his work. In an earlier book, *The Decline of Imperial Russia* (New York, 1952), Seton-Watson covers much the same period (this book began with the emancipation of the serfs), but on the basis of less far-ranging research. Sergei Pushkarev, *The Emergence of Modern Russia 1801–1917* (New York, 1963) covers the same ground, also with impressive factual material, from the point of view of a Russian reformist in exile. His work is the most up-to-date and comprehensive statement of the optimistic case for the destiny of imperial Russia. The bibliography in this book is the most useful one that treats books in Russian as well as Western languages. Another Russian by birth, Michael Florinsky, takes a less sanguine view of the prospects for Russia toward the end of the empire in the second volume of his major two-volume survey entitled *Russia: A History and an Interpretation* (New York, 1953). While not intended as a general survey, Jacob Walkin, *The Rise of Democracy in Prerevolutionary Russia; Political and Social Institutions under the Last Three Tsars* (New York, 1963) may be mentioned here as a work that treats a central theme from the mid-nineteenth century to World War I, taking a strongly optimistic view of the prospects for democratic modernization. This work is particularly valuable for its discussion of some topics often neglected, such as the rise of "voluntary associations" (all manner of nongovernmental, nonparty public organizations) after 1905. Many aspects of political, social, economic, and cultural change during 1905–1914 appear in diverse, excellent essays in Cyril E. Black (ed.), *The Transformation of Russian Society; Aspects of Social Change since 1861* (Cambridge, Mass., 1960).

The post-Stalin outlook in Soviet historiography is represented by A. L. Sidorov (ed.), *Istoriia SSSR, Tom II, 1861–1917, Period kapitalizma (History of the USSR, Vol. II, 1861–1917, The Period of Capitalism)* [1] (Moscow, 1965), from which the selection by Avrekh in the present book is drawn. In English see I. I. Smirnov, (ed.), *Short History of the USSR*, Vol. I (Moscow, 1965), which includes a concise chronological table.

Several general works focus more specifically on the last years of the empire. Richard Charques, *The Twilight of Imperial Russia* (London, 1958) is evocative and skillfully written, while Lionel Kochan, *Russia in Revolution, 1890–1917* is a somewhat more impressive synthesis of a wide variety of material, presented smoothly and economically. Both take a generally pessimistic view of the condition of the empire. An exceedingly optimistic interpretation of the same period, from which the present book draws an excerpt, is S. S. Oldenburg', *Tsarstvovanie Imperatora Nikolai II (The Reign of Emperor Nicholas II)* (Belgrade, 1939, and Munich, 1949). This book is not primarily a life of the last tsar. No satisfactory biography of Nicholas II exists, although Robert Massie, *Nicholas and Alexandra* (New York, 1967) enjoyed great popularity.

Whereas the preceding surveys start well before 1905 and conclude with the Revolution of 1917, some other general books begin with the period around the turn of the century and consider the years 1905–1914 as the prologue to Soviet Russian history. Donald Treadgold, *Twentieth Century Russia* (Chicago, 1959) is a highly informative survey of this sort, while Theodore H. Von Laue, *Why Lenin? Why Stalin?* (Philadelphia, 1964) is a concise, stimulating interpretive essay, which sees Communism as a response to the stresses of modernization, and argues that they were beyond the strength of the imperial regime.

Moving now to the Revolution of 1905, one may start with the bulkiest publication, edited by A. M. Pankratova and others, bearing the general title *Revoliutsiia 1905–1907 gg. v Rossii.*

---

[1] In the following pages Russian titles are translated into English in parentheses when there is no available translation of the whole book in English.

Dokumenty i materialy (The Revolution of 1905–1907 in Russia. Documents and Materials) (Moscow, 1955–1961). The seventeen volumes in this Bolshevik monument bear various titles. In its reverence for this revolution, the Communist party of the Soviet Union has encouraged the publication of vast quantities of books and articles, many of them dealing with the revolution in this or that locality. In English the best introduction to the Soviet point of view is still probably the second volume of M. N. Pokrovsky's *Brief History of Russia* (London 1933; Orono, Maine, 1968), much of which is devoted to 1905–1907. His approach to Russian history was condemned in Stalin's era and partly rehabilitated afterward. An example of the more interesting recent Soviet research on this revolution is L. K. Erman, *Intelligentsiia v pervoi russkoi revoliutsii (The Intelligentsia in the First Russian Revolution)* (Moscow, 1966).

Sidney Harcave has attempted to provide a general account of the revolution to the end of 1905 in *First Blood; The Russian Revolution of 1905* (New York, 1964) and in many respects he has succeeded in reducing the complexity of the year to manageable proportions. Some important questions receive scant attention here, however—the role of the Soviets of Workers' Deputies, for example. This is the subject of the first portion of Oscar Anweiler, *Die Rätebewegung in Russland 1905–1921* (Leiden, 1958). Two participants in the Revolution who have, many years apart, written books that are concerned with the soviets, especially in St. Petersburg, are L. D. Trotsky, *1905* (written in 1908–1909; 4th Russian edition 1922; never translated into English) and Solomon M. Schwarz, *The Russian Revolution of 1905. The Workers' Movement and the Formation of Bolshevism and Menshevism* (Chicago, 1967). A celebrated episode in the Revolution has received a brisk summation in Richard Hough, *The Potemkin Mutiny* (Englewood Cliffs, N.J., 1960). Important works on or from the government side of the barricades are sparse, but the latter part of *The Memoirs of Count Witte* (New York, 1921) deals with the first Russian premier's version of his experiences. This should be supplemented by Theodore Von Laue's article "Count Witte and the 1905 Revolution," *The American Slavic and*

East European Review, XVII, 1 (February, 1958), 25–46.

The political history of the Duma period has been the subject of fairly extensive writing. The fundamental source for research is naturally the official records of the representative institutions: *Gosudarstvennaia Duma, Stenograficheskie ochety Dumy I, II, III, IV sozyvov* (St. Petersburg, 1906–1917) *(State Duma Stenographic Report of the First, Second, Third, and Fourth Dumas).* (Reproduced by Readex Microprint Corp. in "Russian Historical Sources," first series.) Also in Russian, one has a useful anthology that includes such documents as the Bulygin Manifesto, the October Manifesto, and the Fundamental Laws on the Duma: F. I. Kalinychev, (ed.), *Gosudarstvennaia Duma v Rossii. Sbornik dokumentakh i materialakh (The State Duma in Russia. A Collection of Documents and Materials)* (Moscow, 1967). A. I. Avrekh, has established himself as the principal authority on this period among Soviet historians, his main work being *Stolypin i tret'ia duma (Stolypin and the Third Duma)* (Moscow, 1968). Among his other writings, a major article entitled *"Tret'eiunskaia monarkhiia i rabochii vopros"* ("The June Third Monarchy and the Labor Question"), *Istoriia SSSR,* 1966, no. 1, 42–69, merits special attention. But the policies of the Duma monarchy have not been very high on the priority list of Soviet historical research.

Most of the writing on this has come from Russian émigré or non-Russian scholars. A "conservative-liberal" overview of the problem is provided in *Geschichte des Liberalismus in Russland (History of Liberalism in Russia)* (Frankfurt, 1957) by V. Leontowitsch, a jurist by background who is more concerned with the establishment of a rule of law in Russia than egalitarianism. His work is rare in that it gives some serious attention to the Council of State. A much shorter interpretation of the liberal dilemma in Russia during the Duma is Michael Karpovich, "Two Types of Russian Liberalism: Maklakov and Miliukov," in Ernest J. Simmons (ed.), *Continuity and Change in Russian and Soviet Thought* (New York, 1955). Miliukov is the subject of a major political biography by Thomas Riha, *A Russian European; Paul Miliukov in Russian Politics* (Notre Dame, Ind., 1969), and

has left his own partisan *Political Memoirs 1905–1917,* edited by Arthur P. Mendel (Ann Arbor, Mich., 1967). Maklakov's memoirs concerning *The First State Duma* (Bloomington, Ill., 1964) are also available.

In the absence of any extensive, general study of the Duma as an institution, several specialized articles are valuable: Warren B. Walsh, "Political Parties of the Russian Duma," *Journal of Modern History,* XXII (June, 1950), 144–150; and C. J. Smith, "The Third State Duma: An Analytical Profile," *The Russian Review,* XVII, 3 (July, 1958), 201–210. A meticulous appraisal of popular response to the electoral law of June 3, 1907, is given by Alfred Levin in "The Russian Voter in the Elections for the Third Duma," *Slavic Review,* XXI, 4 (December, 1962), 660–677.

He has also written an important analysis of one of the reasons for the failure of the Second Duma as an effective representative body: *The Second Duma: A Study of the Social-Democratic Party and the Russian Constitutional Experiment* (New Haven, Conn., 1940).

A potentially important aspect of the new politics in Russia after 1905 is the emergence of the "radical right," which has received little attention. The most important single writing on this theme is Hans Rogger, "Was There a Russian Fascism? The Union of the Russian People," *Journal of Modern History,* XXXVI, 4 (December, 1964), 398–415. There was a juncture of the extreme Right groups and the elements in the imperial government on one particularly odious policy—antisemitism. The most flagrant attempt by the government to utilize the potential power of anti-Jewish feeling was the prosecution of one Mendel Beilis on the charge of committing ritual murder. Rogger has analyzed government involvement in the case in "The Beilis Case: Anti-Semitism and Politics in the Reign of Nicholas II," *Slavic Review,* XXV, 4 (December 1966), 615–629. A general account of the case is Maurice Samuel, *Blood Accusation* (New York, 1966).

The actual administration of the Russian empire in its last prewar years has received little attention in any country, the bureaucracy not attracting much sympathy from either Communist or non-Communist historians. Its leading figure, Premier Stolypin, still awaits his biographer, although he has been the subject of several scholarly articles, of which the most distinguished and general is Alfred Levin, "P. A. Stolypin: A Political Appraisal," *Journal of Modern History*, XXXVII, 4 (December, 1965), 445–463. A careful study of his policy toward the zemtsvo system, which was of special interest to Stolypin, is M. S. Conroy, "Stolypin's Attitude toward Local Self-Government," *Slavonic and East European Review*, XLVI, 107 (July, 1968), 446–461. Some of the premier's later difficulties in the politics of bureaucracy are discussed in Edward Chmielewski's two articles, "Stolypin's Last Crisis," *California Slavic Studies*, III (1964), 95-126, and "Stolypin and the Russian Ministerial Crisis of 1909," *California Slavic Studies*, 4 (1967), 1–38. Two articles that display an unusual understanding of the character of the imperial bureaucracy in this period are George L. Yaney, "Some Aspects of the Imperial Russian Government on the Eve of the First World War," *Slavonic and East European Review*, XLIII, 1 (December, 1964), 68-90, and Alfred Levin, "Russian Bureaucratic Opinion in the Wake of the 1905 Revolution" (in English), *Jahrbücher für Geschichte Osteuropas*, N. F. Band 11, Heft 4 (1963), 1-12. Two moderately apologetic memoirs by a former premier and a deputy-minister respectively are, V. N. Kokovtsov, *Out of My Past.* (Stanford, Calif., 1935), and V. I. Gurko, *Figures and Features of the Past; Government and Opinion in the Reign of Nicholas II* (Stanford, Calif., 1939). Another interesting memoir is Mary P. Bock, *Vospominaniia o moem otse P. A. Stolypine (Memoirs of My Father P. A. Stolypin)* (New York, 1953). The lurid circumstances surrounding his assassination are examined by George Tokmakoff, "Stolypin's Assassin." *Slavic Review*, XXIV, 2 (June, 1965), 314-321.

The historical writing on Russian socialism in 1905–1914 deserves separate comment because it is exceptionally abundant and is often approached not so much as an aspect of this period as part of the whole history of the movement. The field of study is a veritable industry in the USSR, and for the purposes of this book one need only list the current, highly contentious text from which one part of this book was excerpted, *History of the Communist Party of the Soviet Union* (Moscow, 1960), and the weightier, equally contentious *Istoriia Kommunisticheskoi Partii Sovetkogo Soiuza, Tom vtoroi, Partiia Bol'shevikov v bor'be za sverzhenie tsarizma 1904 —Fevral' 1917 goda (History of the Communist Party of the Soviet Union*, second volume, *The Party of Bolsheviks in the Struggle for the Overthrow of Tsarism 1904-February, 1917)* (Moscow, 1966).

The principal general work on Communist party history written in the West is Leonard Schapiro, *The Communist Party of the Soviet Union* (New York, 1960). The early years of the party, culminating with the revolution of 1905–1907, receive more detailed treatment in J. L. H. Keep, *The Rise of Social Democracy in Russia* (New York, 1963). Two relatively detailed treatments of Lenin as the center of the movement are Adam B. Ulam, *The Bolsheviks: The Intellectual, Personal and Political History of the Origins of Russian Communism* (New York, 1965), and Bertram D. Wolfe, *Three Who Made a Revolution* (New York, 1948), which covers the careers of Lenin, Trotsky and Stalin to 1914. Donald W. Treadgold, *Lenin and His Rivals* (New York, 1955) is particularly notable because it combines discussion of the Bolsheviks with treatment of other branches of Russian socialism and liberalism. Much may be learned about the Mensheviks in Israel Getzler, *Martov; A Political Biography of a Russian Social Democrat* (New York, 1967). The best introduction to the role of trade unions in the Russian labor movement is S. P. Turin, *From Peter the Great to Lenin. A History of the Russian Labor Movement with Special Reference to Trade Unions* (2d ed., London, 1968), a large part of which deals with 1905-1917.

The peasant question is the subject of several important works, most of which were written quite a few years ago. The latter part of Geroid T. Robinson's well-known work, *Rural Russia under the Old Regime* (New York, 1929) treats the Revolution of 1905 and the Stolypin reforms, considering both the peasantry and the nobility. In *The Russian Peasant Movement 1906–1917* (London, 1937), Launcelot A. Owen discusses the peasant and agrarian reform, not in connection with the rural upper class but in relation to Lenin and his party. Both Robinson and Owen emphasize the grave difficulties in the later em-

pire. Soviet historians take an even more negative view of the agrarian situation. See, for example, A. B. Shapkarin (ed.), *Krest'ianskoe dviz-
henie v Rossii iiun' 1907 g.—Iiul' 1914 g. Sbornik
dokumentov. (The Peasant Movement in Russia, June
1907–July 1914. A Collection of Documents)* (Moscow, 1960), which offers varied evidence of peasant discontent in the period of the Stolypin
reform.

A much more optimistic analysis of this reform appears in George Pavlovsky, *Agricultural
Russia on the Eve of the Revolution* (London, 1930),
which takes a mainly economic approach to the
problem, considering productivity and technique in various branches of agriculture. This
outlook is shared by several agrarian experts
writing in postrevolutionary emigration: Alexis
N. Antsiferov, et al., *Russian Agriculture During the
War* (New Haven, Conn., 1930), which in large
measure is devoted to the harmful impact of the
war on what is presented as a fairly good situation. Antsiferov and Eugene M. Kayden present another dimension of the optimistic appraisal of the agricultural situation in *The
Cooperative Movement in Russia During the War*
(New Haven, Conn., 1929). As they show, this
major development was not by any means
limited to agriculture.

Still another dimension of the positive appraisal of the agrarian situation is the relatively
prosperous agriculture that developed in Siberia after the government began to assist migration. This is discussed with considerable force
and concision in Treadgold, *The Great Siberian
Migration* (Princeton, N. J., 1957). The same
writer seeks to debunk one common interpretation of Stolypin's agrarian policy in "Was Stolypin in Favor of Kulaks?" *Slavic Review*, XVII,
1 (February, 1965), 1–14.

The most influential American writing on industrial development in Russia before 1917 is
probably W. W. Rostow's small book, *The Stages
of Economic Growth* (Cambridge, Mass., 1960).
While his book does not deal in detail with the
years 1905–1914, Rostow's general thesis that
prewar Russia was well started on the path to
industrialization is directly relevant to these
years. Some important background statistics
and commentary, are found in Alexander
Gerschenkron's essay, "The Rate of Industrial

Growth in Russia since 1885," *The Journal of
Economic History*, Supplement VII, 1947. The
optimistic appraisal of the first decades of Russian industrialization has come under sharp criticism from some non-Communist scholars who
have made close studies of the period. Theodore H. Von Laue has written *Sergei Witte and
the Industrialization of Russia* (New York, 1963),
which ends in 1903 with the dismissal of Witte
as minister of finance. Jurgen Nötzold takes a
somewhat longer view in his *Wirtschaftspolitische
Alternativen der Entwicklung Russlands in der Ära
Witte und Stolypin* (Berlin, 1966).

Roger Portal's contribution to *The Cambridge
Economic History of Europe*, Vol. VI (London,
1965) on "The Industrialization of Russia" is a
valuable summation.

Additional statistical and other descriptive
material appears in Margaret Miller, *The Economic Development of Russia 1905–1914 with Special
Reference to Trade, Industry and Finance* (2d ed.,
London, 1967). Her study stresses state participation in all phases of economic life. Private
industrial leadership is a vital aspect of Russian
modernization that has been sorely neglected.
There is however one valuable article: Ruth
Roosa, "Russian Industrialists Look to the Future: Thoughts on Economic Development
1906–1917," in John S. Curtiss (ed.), *Essays in
Russian and Soviet History* (New York, 1963). A
Soviet interpretation reflecting the party line in
the Stalin period is Peter I. Lyashchenko, *History of the National Economy of Russia to the 1917
Revolution* (New York, 1949); chapters 31–37
deal with the period with which the present
book is concerned. One of his theses is that
prewar Russia had become a "semi-colony" in
its relations with the West. This view has been
modified since Stalin died. The prewar situation
of Russia is no longer considered semi-colo-
nial, as is suggested by various essays in the
anthology edited by A. L. Sidorov, *Ob osobennos-
tiakh imperializma v Rossii (Concerning the Peculiar-
ities of Imperialism in Russia)* (Moscow, 1963).

It would be satisfying to be able to list a good
variety of works on the social-cultural history of
Russia on the eve of the war, but the immediately relevant items are sparse. While there are
numerous works of literary and artistic criticism,
none of these really relates the formal cul-

ture to the problem of a general social-cultural crisis (if there was one). Two general introductions to the arts in Russia at this time are Marc Slonim, *From Chekhov to the Revolution; Russian Literature 1900–1917* (New York, 1962), and Camilla Gray, *The Great Experiment: Russian Art 1863-1922*, illustrated (New York, 1962), which deals with the brilliant flowering of modern painting in Russia. There is much interesting comment, in a far broader context, in James Billington, *The Icon and the Axe, An Interpretive History of Russian Culture* (New York, 1966). The history of ideas, which has been rather extensively studied with respect to most of the imperial age in Russia, offers little. However, the reader may turn to Leonard B. Schapiro, "The *Vekhi* Group and the Mystique of Revolution," *The Slavonic and East European Review,* XXXIV, 1 (December, 1955), 56-76, and may find some interesting suggestions in essays by Pipes and Leopold Haimson in Richard Pipes (ed.), *The Russian Intelligentsia* (New York, 1961). Education, in which development was unquestionably rapid, may be approached in D. M. Odinetz and P. J. Novgorodtsov, *Russian Schools and Universities During the War* (New Haven, Conn., 1930). Two dissimilar appraisals of the position of the Russian Orthodox Church around this time are John S. Curtiss (rather negative), *Church and State in Russia: The Last Years of the Empire* (New York, 1940) and Nicolas Zernov (optimistic) *The Russian Religious Renaissance of the Twentieth Century* (London, 1963).

Finally the *Slavic Review* published an exceedingly interesting essay by Leopold Haimson, followed by a lively debate concerning the destiny of imperial Russia as it appeared on the eve of World War I. Unfortunately, this material is too lengthy for inclusion in the present book, and it is almost impossible to condense satisfactorily. However, the following essays are particularly recommended to readers of the present book as an extension of its purpose: Leopold Haimson, "The Problem of Social Stability in Urban Russia, 1905–1917," Part I, *Slavic Review,* XXIII, 4 (December, 1964), 619–642; Part II, *ibid.,* XXIV, 1 (March 1965), 1–22; Arthur P. Mendel, "Peasant and Worker on the Eve of the First World War," *ibid.,* 23–33; Theodore H. Von Laue, "The Chances for Liberal Constitutionalism," *ibid.,* 34–46; Haimson, "Reply," *ibid.,* 47–65; George L. Yaney, "Social Stability in Prerevolutionary Russia: a Critical Note," XXIV, 4 (September, 1965), 520–527; Alfred Levin, "More on Social Stability," XXV, 1 (March, 1966), 149-154.

As the present book was going to press, an especially important collection of essays on the major themes from the reign of Nicholas II was published under the editorship of Theofanis G. Stavrou, *Russia under the Last Tsar* (Minneapolis, 1969).